12th Workshop on Graph-Based Methods for Natural Language Processing (TextGraphs-12)

New Orleans, Louisiana, USA
6 June 2018

ISBN: 978-1-5108-6367-5

NAACL HLT 2018

**Graph-Based Methods for
Natural Language Processing**

Proceedings of the Twelfth Workshop

June 6, 2018
New Orleans, Louisiana

Introduction

Welcome to TextGraphs, the Workshop on Graph-Based Methods for Natural Language Processing. The twelfth edition of our workshop is being organized on June 6, 2018, in conjunction with the 16th Annual Conference of the North American Chapter of the Association for Computational Linguistics: Human Language Technologies, being held in New Orleans, Louisiana, USA.

The workshops in the TextGraphs series have published and promoted the synergy between the field of Graph Theory (GT) and Natural Language Processing (NLP) for over a decade. The target audience of our workshop comprises of researchers working on problems related to either Graph Theory or graph-based algorithms applied to Natural Language Processing, social media, and the Semantic Web.

TextGraphs addresses a broad spectrum of research areas within NLP. This is because, besides traditional NLP applications like parsing, word sense disambiguation, semantic role labeling, and information extraction, graph-based solutions also target web-scale applications like information propagation in social networks, rumor proliferation, e-reputation, language dynamics learning, and future events prediction. Following this tradition, this year's TextGraphs also presents research from diverse topics such as lexical and computational semantics, text clustering and classification, and text compresion and summarization, to name a few.

The selection process was competitive – we received 17 submissions (9 long and 8 short submissions) and accepted for presentation 8 of them (5 long and 3 short papers), resulting in the overall acceptance rate of 47%.

We are pleased to have two excellent invited speakers for this year's event. We thank Gabor Melli and Maximilian Nickel for their enthusiastic acceptance of our invitation. Finally, we are thankful to the members of the program committee for their valuable and high quality reviews. All submissions have benefited from their expert feedback. Their timely contribution was the basis for accepting an excellent list of papers and making the twelfth edition of TextGraphs a success.

Goran Glavaš, Swapna Somasundaran, Martin Riedl, and Ed Hovy
TextGraphs-12 Organizers
April 2018

Organizers:

Goran Glavaš, University of Mannheim, Germany
Swapna Somasundaran, Educational Testing Service, Princeton, USA
Martin Riedl, University of Stuttgart, Germany
Eduard Hovy, Carnegie Mellon University, USA

Program Committee:

Željko Agić, IT University Copenhagen, Denmark
Chris Biemann, University of Hamburg, Germany
Tomáš Brychcín, University of West Bohemia, Czech Republic
Flavio Massimiliano Cecchini, University of Milano-Bicocca, Italy
Tanmoy Chakraborty, IIIT Delhi, India
Monojit Choudhury, Microsoft Research Lab, India
Stefano Faralli, Università degli Studi di Roma Unitelma Sapienza, Italy
Michael Flor, Educational Testing Service, USA
Marc Franco Salvador, Symanto Group, Germany
Carlos Gomez-Rodriguez, University of A. Coruña, Spain
Binod Gyawali, Educational Testing Service, USA
Tomáš Hercig, University of West Bohemia, Czech Republic
Anne Lauscher, University of Mannheim, Germany
Nikola Ljubešić, University of Zagreb, Croatia
Héctor Martínez Alonso, Inria & University Paris Diderot, France
Gabor Melli, PlayStation Network, USA
Mohsen Mesgar, Heidelberg Institute for Theoretical Studies, Germany
Rada Mihalcea, University of Michigan, USA
Alessandro Moschitti, University of Trento, Italy
Animesh Mukherjee, IIT Kharagpur, India
Matthew Mulholland, Educational Testing Service, USA
Federico Nanni, University of Mannheim, Germany
Vivi Nastase, University of Heidelberg, Germany
Alexander Panchenko, University of Hamburg, Germany
Simone Paolo Ponzetto, University of Mannheim, Germany
Jan Wira Gotama Putra, Tokyo Institute of Technology, Japan
Steffen Remus, Univeristät Hamburg, Germany
Brian Riordan, Educational Testing Services, USA
Stephan Roller, UT Austin, USA
Natalie Schluter, IT University Copenhagen, Denmark
Khalil Sima'an, University of Amsterdam, Netherlands
Josef Steinberger, University of West Bohemia, Czech Republic
Kateryna Tymosenko, University of Trento, Italy
Dmitry Ustalov, University of Mannheim, Germany
Aline Villavicencio, F. University of Rio Grande do Sul, Brazil
Ivan Vulić, University of Cambridge, United Kingdom
Fabio Massimo Zanzotto, "Tor vergata" University of Rome, Italy
Xiang Zhao, National University of Defense Technology, China

Invited Speakers:

Gabor Melli, Playstation Network, USA
Maximilian Nickel, Massachusetts Institute of Technology, USA

Table of Contents

Scientific Discovery as Link Prediction in Influence and Citation Graphs
Fan Luo, Marco A. Valenzuela-Escárcega, Gus Hahn-Powell and Mihai Surdeanu 1

Efficient Generation and Processing of Word Co-occurrence Networks Using corpus2graph
Zheng Zhang, Pierre Zweigenbaum and Ruiqing Yin 7

Multi-hop Inference for Sentence-level TextGraphs: How Challenging is Meaningfully Combining Information for Science Question Answering?
Peter Jansen 12

Multi-Sentence Compression with Word Vertex-Labeled Graphs and Integer Linear Programming
Elvys Linhares Pontes, Stéphane Huet, Thiago Gouveia da Silva, Andréa carneiro Linhares and Juan-Manuel Torres-Moreno 18

Large-scale spectral clustering using diffusion coordinates on landmark-based bipartite graphs
Khiem Pham and Guangliang Chen 28

Efficient Graph-based Word Sense Induction by Distributional Inclusion Vector Embeddings
Haw-Shiuan Chang, Amol Agrawal, Ananya Ganesh, Anirudha Desai, Vinayak Mathur, Alfred Hough and Andrew McCallum 38

Fusing Document, Collection and Label Graph-based Representations with Word Embeddings for Text Classification
Konstantinos Skianis, Fragkiskos Malliaros and Michalis Vazirgiannis 49

Embedding Text in Hyperbolic Spaces
Bhuwan Dhingra, Christopher Shallue, Mohammad Norouzi, Andrew Dai and George Dahl 59

Conference Program

Wednesday, June 6, 2018

9:00–9:10 *Opening Remarks*

Session 1

9:10–10:10 *Invited talk: Neural domain-specific wikification*
Gabor Melli

10:10–10:30 *Scientific Discovery as Link Prediction in Influence and Citation Graphs*
Fan Luo, Marco A. Valenzuela-Escárcega, Gus Hahn-Powell and Mihai Surdeanu

10:30–11:00 *Coffee break*

Session 2

11:00–11:20 *Efficient Generation and Processing of Word Co-occurrence Networks Using corpus2graph*
Zheng Zhang, Pierre Zweigenbaum and Ruiqing Yin

11:20–11:40 *Multi-hop Inference for Sentence-level TextGraphs: How Challenging is Meaningfully Combining Information for Science Question Answering?*
Peter Jansen

11:40–12:05 *Multi-Sentence Compression with Word Vertex-Labeled Graphs and Integer Linear Programming*
Elvys Linhares Pontes, Stéphane Huet, Thiago Gouveia da Silva, Andréa carneiro Linhares and Juan-Manuel Torres-Moreno

12:05–14:05 *Lunch break*

Session 3

14:05–15:05 *Invited talk: Hierarchical Representation Learning on Graphs*
Maximilian Nickel

15:05–15:30 *Large-scale spectral clustering using diffusion coordinates on landmark-based bipartite graphs*
Khiem Pham and Guangliang Chen

15:30–16:00 *Coffee break*

Session 4

16:00–16:25 *Efficient Graph-based Word Sense Induction by Distributional Inclusion Vector Embeddings*
Haw-Shiuan Chang, Amol Agrawal, Ananya Ganesh, Anirudha Desai, Vinayak Mathur, Alfred Hough and Andrew McCallum

16:25–16:50 *Fusing Document, Collection and Label Graph-based Representations with Word Embeddings for Text Classification*
Konstantinos Skianis, Fragkiskos Malliaros and Michalis Vazirgiannis

16:50–17:15 *Embedding Text in Hyperbolic Spaces*
Bhuwan Dhingra, Christopher Shallue, Mohammad Norouzi, Andrew Dai and George Dahl

17:15–17.30 *Closing remarks*

Scientific Discovery as Link Prediction in Influence and Citation Graphs

Fan Luo   Marco Valenzuela-Escárcega   Gus Hahn-Powell   Mihai Surdeanu
University of Arizona, Tucson, AZ, USA
{fanluo, marcov, hahnpowell, msurdeanu}@email.arizona.edu

Abstract

We introduce a machine learning approach for the identification of "white spaces" in scientific knowledge. Our approach addresses this task as link prediction over a graph that contains over 2M influence statements such as "CTCF activates FOXA1", which were automatically extracted using open-domain machine reading. We model this prediction task using graph-based features extracted from the above influence graph, as well as from a citation graph that captures scientific communities. We evaluated the proposed approach through backtesting. Although the data is heavily unbalanced (50 times more negative examples than positives), our approach predicts which influence links will be discovered in the "near future" with a F1 score of 27 points, and a mean average precision of 68%.

1 Introduction

The amount of scientific knowledge that is publicly available has increased dramatically in the past few years. For example, PubMed, a search engine of biomedical publications,[1] now indexes over 25 million papers, 17 million of which were published between 1990 and the present. This information overload yields two critical problems. First, this exceeds the human capacity to aggregate and interpret the fragments of knowledge published in these papers, which may result in existing solutions to critical problems being overlooked. Swanson (1986) described this problem as "undiscovered public knowledge". Second, this vast amount of available information complicates the identification of "**white spaces**" in science, i.e., topics that are insufficiently studied and may lead to important scientific discoveries.

While the first problem has been addressed recently with efforts that combine machine reading and assembly with existing data analysis algorithms (Valenzuela-Escarcega et al., 2017; Poon et al., 2015, inter alia), the second problem is largely unstudied.

In this work we propose a first enabling step towards addressing the problem of white space discovery from literature (Sebastian et al., 2017; Cameron, 2014) with an approach inspired from the field of link prediction (Liben-Nowell and Kleinberg, 2007; Leskovec et al., 2010). In particular, our method operates over two graphs: (a) a graph of positive/negative influence relations such as the relation "CTCF activates FOXA1" between the two proteins, which were extracted using an existing, open-domain machine reading tool (Hahn-Powell et al., 2017) from over 100K biomedical publications[2]; and (b) the citation graph between the corresponding papers where these findings were published. The proposed approach approximates the task of white space discovery by predicting new influence relations that do not exist in the influence graph at a given time (hence the white space) but will emerge in future (thus somebody identified the missing knowledge as important).

The contributions of this work are:

(1) We propose a novel machine learning (ML) framework for this prediction task that uses features extracted from both the influence graph (e.g., the connectivity of relevant concepts in the graph) and the citation graph (e.g., the affinity between related influence relations measured by membership to communities in citation space).

(2) We evaluate the proposed method on an influence graph extracted from over 100K pa-

---

[2] These relations were extracted using a grammar that identifies causal statements in text. However, we prefer the term "influence" to "causality" in this work because here we simply rely on the text and do not demonstrate that these findings are truly causal.

Proceedings of the Twelfth Workshop on Graph-Based Methods for Natural Language Processing (TextGraphs-12), pages 1–6
New Orleans, Louisiana, June 6, 2018. ©2018 Association for Computational Linguistics

pers, which contains 1,564,748 concepts (e.g., "astrocytes", "proinflammatory cytokines") and 2,395,944 influence relations (e.g., "VEGF increases Akt"). Our method obtains an F1 score of 27 points and a mean average precision of 68%. This outperforms considerably methods that extract features only from one of the two graphs.

(3) To promote future work on this topic, we release a dataset containing both the influence and the citation graphs used in this paper, available at: `https://github.com/clulab/releases/tree/master/textgraphs2018-discovery`.

2 Data

As mentioned, the primary graph this method operates on is a graph of influence relations extracted from a corpus of 119,667 PubMed Open Access publications. These papers were previously selected to be relevant to the topic of children's health, which spans multiple domains, and includes issues such as stunting, wasting, and malnutrition.

All these papers were processed using the machine reading and assembly software of Hahn-Powell et al. (2017). In order to address the multi-domain nature of the children's health, Hahn-Powell et al. followed the OpenIE-style approach of Banko et al. (2007) for entity extraction by considering expanded noun phrases as a coarse approximation of the concepts relevant to the topic. For event extraction, the authors adapted a subset of REACH grammars (Valenzuela-Escarcega et al., 2017) from the biomolecular domain that capture influence statements (e.g., positive and negative regulations). The adaptation removed selectional restrictions on the arguments of each event predicate. That is, they extract any lexicalized variation of "A causes B" where A and B are concepts identified in the entity extraction step. For example, when processing the sentence "Chronic infection may lead to malnutrition and malabsorption", the system extracts the following entities: "Chronic infection", "malnutrition", and "malabsorption". In this particular case, the extracted entities participate in two `promotes` relations: the first between "Chronic infection" and "malnutrition", and the second between "Chronic infection" and "malabsorption".

This machine reading approach was used to read the entire content of these publications (including abstract and body of paper). To reduce

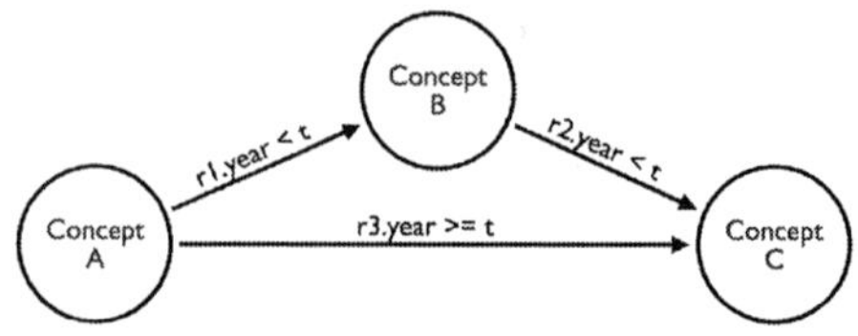

Figure 1: Intuition of the backtesting framework: we predict if links such as A → C will be added to the influence graph after time t, using information that exists before time t such as A → B, and B → C. Setting $t = 2012$ yields 5,015 positive examples, i.e., A → C links that were added after 2012, and 274,251 negative examples, i.e., A → C links that were not added to the graph between 2012 and the end of 2017.

noise we kept only relations extracted at least twice, and which occur between concepts with an inverse document frequency (IDF) larger than 1. The resulting influence graph (IG) contains 1,564,748 distinct nodes, connected by 2,395,944 influence relations.

Each match to these rules produces a directed influence relation[3] that encodes polarity (i.e., increase or decrease). Finally, the relation instances are then consolidated through a conservative deduplication procedure.

Because the hypotheses studied in these publications are generally expressed using causal language, we believe this influence graph (IG) captures the essence of the scientific knowledge in this domain.

The above IG is accompanied by a citation graph (CG), which contains outgoing citations from the above papers, at a total of 5,523,759 citation links.

We model the discovery of important white spaces in this knowledge base as link prediction: we predict which influence links will be added to the IG after time t, using only information available before time t. We believe this is a reasonable approximation for the discovery of important white spaces in science knowledge: influence links that will be added in the future indicate that somebody identified the missing information to be important enough to be studied and published. To limit search space, in this work we focus on the prediction of A → C influence links, when A → B and B → C exist in the graph before time t, for at least one node B. Figure 1 visualizes this procedure.

---

[3]It should be noted that this approach only reads such statements from publications, and does not attempt to verify these findings directly through separate modeling. In other words, the authors statements are assumed to be correct.

t (year)	positive	negative
2017	-	998,586
2016	319	979,709
2015	1,706	881,689
2014	3,767	696,406
2013	5,208	481,671
2012	**5,015**	**274,251**
2011	3,741	151,460
2010	2,448	73,226
2009	1,521	36,839
2008	782	16,372
2007	444	7,843

Table 1: Total number of positive and negative examples for different values of the threshold t.

	Positive Examples	Negative Examples
Training	3,011	164,551
Development	1,002	54,850
Testing	1,002	54,850

Table 2: Number of positive and negative examples in the training, development, and testing partitions.

Note that transitivity cannot be assumed to be true in this graph due to the fact that influence relations extracted from text usually oversimplify complex causal processes. We show in Section 4 that relying on this transitivity assumption leads to poor predictions.

We implemented the above task through backtesting. That is, we look at an arbitrary point in time in the past (t), and create positive training examples from A → C links that were added to IG after t. Similarly, we create negative examples from A → C links that do not appear between time t and the present. Note that these negative examples are an approximation: some of these may correspond to inventions that will be published at future dates that are beyond the coverage of our dataset. In this paper we used $t = 2012$. This choice of t is justified in Table 1, which shows the distribution of positive and negative examples for different values of t. We chose $t = 2012$ because this provided a large enough number of positive examples, while still maintaining a realistic distribution of negative examples.

The dataset was split into training/development/testing as indicated in Table 2, using a 60-20-20% split. During the partitioning, we made sure that identical influence links coming from different papers are all allocated to the same partition.

3 Approach

We model link prediction as i.i.d. classification on the above dataset, exploring multiple classifiers in Section 4. One key contribution of this work is the feature set used by these classifiers, which is summarized in Table 3. At a higher level, these features capture the connectivity of both the IG and CG around a candidate link, under the assumption that the more connected the corresponding graph is around A and C, the more likely it is that the link $A \rightarrow C$ will be discovered in the near future. In particular, from the IG we extract the in- and out-degrees of the source/destination nodes, and statistics from the path(s) connecting the two nodes such as the length of the shortest path connecting the source and destination nodes, or the inverse document frequency (IDF) scores of the nodes on these paths.

From the CG, we derive features based on the probabilities that papers containing $A \rightarrow B$ ($\mathbf{p}_{A \rightarrow B}$) and $B \rightarrow C$ ($\mathbf{p}_{B \rightarrow C}$) belong to the same community/ies, motivated by the idea that discoveries are easier to be made if the individual fragments that form the puzzle ($A \rightarrow B$ and $B \rightarrow C$ here) come from the same or related discipline(s). We model the probability that two papers, $p1$ and $p2$, belong to the same community $P(p1, p2)$ using two configurations of the Coda community detection algorithm (Yang et al., 2014), one in which detects 100 communities, and another where it detects 300. Because influence links may be reported in more than one paper, we derived the max/min/avg $P(p_{A \rightarrow B}, p_{B \rightarrow C})$ features, which are computed across all possible combinations of papers $p_{A \rightarrow B}$ and $p_{B \rightarrow C}$.

Lastly, we add a series of features (bottom part of Table 3) extracted from the collection of biomedical publications used in these experiments, such as IDF scores of the relevant concept nodes and the counts for the number of papers that mention a given influence link.

4 Results

Table 4 lists the results of several classifiers on the test partition,[4] compared against two baselines. The first baseline randomly creates positive links following the distribution of positive examples from the training partition. The second base-

---

[4] All classifier hyper parameters were tuned on the development partition. All classification results were averaged over 5 runs.

Feature Name	Description
C_A.outdegree	Out-degree of source concept node A, i.e., number of influence relations starting on A
C_A.indegree	In-degree of source concept node A, i.e., number of influence relations ending on A
C_C.outdegree	Out-degree of destination concept node C
C_C.indegree	In-degree of destination concept node C
$C_{inbetween}$.outdegree	Out-degree of nodes in all the shortest paths that connect A to C but do not pass through B
$C_{inbetween}$.indegree	In-degree of nodes in all the shortest paths that connect A to C but do not pass through B
shortest_path_length	The length of the shortest path that connects A to C but does not pass through B; 0 if no such path exists
shortest_path_count	The number of shortest paths that connect A to C but do not pass through B
$C_{inbetween}$.avg-idf	Average inverse document frequency (IDF) of nodes in-between A and C in all the above shortest paths
$r_{inbetween}$.avg-seen	Average number of papers containing an edge in the above shortest paths
max P($p_{A \to B}$,$p_{B \to C}$)	Maximum probability of papers $p_{A \to B}$ and $p_{B \to C}$ being related based on their membership to multi-communities detected by the Coda algorithm; p_r refers to any paper that contains influence relation r.
min P($p_{A \to B}$,$p_{B \to C}$)	Minimum probability of papers $p_{A \to B}$ and $p_{B \to C}$ being related based on their membership to multi-communities detected by the Coda algorithm
avg P($p_{A \to B}$,$p_{B \to C}$)	Average probability of papers $p_{A \to B}$ and $p_{B \to C}$ being related based on their membership to multi-communities detected by the Coda algorithm
Jaccard($\mathbf{p}_{A \to B}$,$\mathbf{p}_{B \to C}$)	Jaccard similarity between the set of papers that contain the link $A \to B$ ($\mathbf{p}_{A \to B}$) and the set of papers that contain $B \to C$ ($\mathbf{p}_{B \to C}$)
Inter-citation ratio	The number of citations between the two sets $\mathbf{p}_{A \to B}$ and $\mathbf{p}_{B \to C}$ normalized by the size of the union of the two sets.
C_A.idf	IDF of the lemmatized terms of source concept node A
C_B.idf	IDF of the lemmatized terms of intermediate concept node B
C_C.idf	IDF of the lemmatized terms of destination concept node C
r1.seen	Number of papers that contain the influence relation $A \to B$
r2.seen	Number of papers that contain the influence relation $B \to C$

Table 3: List of features used by the link prediction classifier that classifies the candidate link $A \to C$, given an intermediate node B. The top part of table lists the features derived from the influence graph. The middle part lists features extracted from the citation graph. The bottom part contains features extracted from the collection of papers.

line assumes that all candidate links are positive, i.e., candidate $A \to C$ is always correct if $A \to B$ and $B \to C$ exist for some B.

This table yields several observations. First, the performance of the first (random) baseline is very low, indicating that this is indeed a hard task that is exacerbated by the biased label distribution. Second, the precision of the second baseline is also very low, confirming that the transitive closure assumption is not supported on this realistic influence graph. Third, all classifiers considerably outperform the baseline, indicating that capturing the structure of the IG and CG is indeed indicative of the likelihood that an influence link will be discovered in the near future. Fourth, a linear support vector machines (SVM) classifier did not converge on this data, indicating that, while it is possible to learn a model for this link prediction task, the resulting model is more complex than a linear function. All in all, the best non-linear model (Ad-

	F1	Precision	Recall	P@10	MAP
Baseline (random)	0.02	0.02	0.02	-	-
Baseline (all positive)	0.035	0.018	**1**	-	-
Neural Network	**0.27**	0.398	0.206	0.8	0.537
AdaBoost	0.27	**0.536**	0.178	**0.9**	**0.681**
Random Forest	0.23	0.244	**0.216**	0.5	0.309

Table 4: Unranked scores –precision, recall, and F1– and ranked scores –precision at 10 (P@10), and mean average precision (MAP)– of several classifiers for the prediction of influence links using backtesting at time $t = 2012$. The baseline predicts that every $A \to C$ link will be discovered after time t, if $A \to B$ and $B \to C$ exist before time t.

aBoost) obtained an F1 score of 0.27, an order of magnitude higher than the baseline, and a mean average precision (MAP) of 0.68, indicating that most correct predictions are ranked closer to the top.

Table 5 shows the results of an ablation experiment in which we measured the drop in performance when each feature was individually removed from the full AdaBoost model. This experiment indicates that, importantly, both the influ-

Removed Feature	F1	Precision	Recall
Full model	0.268	0.528	0.176
$- C_A$.outdegree	0.234	0.678	0.14
$- C_A$.indegree	0.246	0.44	0.17
$- C_C$.outdegree	0.214	0.248	0.186
$- C_C$.indegree	0.2	0.232	0.172
$- C_{\text{inbetween}}$.outdegree	0.22	0.272	0.182
$- C_{\text{inbetween}}$.indegree	0.234	0.3	0.192
$- C_{\text{inbetween}}$.avg-idf	0.214	0.272	0.18
$- r_{\text{inbetween}}$.avg-seen	0.23	0.29	0.192
$-$ shortest_path_count	0.222	0.29	0.182
$-$ shortest_path_length	0.204	0.28	0.16
$-$ max $P(p_{A \to B}, p_{B \to C})$ (c=100)	0.226	0.3	0.18
$-$ min $P(p_{A \to B}, p_{B \to C})$ (c=100)	0.228	0.302	0.184
$-$ avg $P(p_{A \to B}, p_{B \to C})$ (c=100)	0.232	0.306	0.186
$-$ max $P(p_{A \to B}, p_{B \to C})$ (c=300)	0.232	0.314	0.182
$-$ min $P(p_{A \to B}, p_{B \to C})$ (c=300)	0.23	0.298	0.18
$-$ avg $P(p_{A \to B}, p_{B \to C})$ (c=300)	0.232	0.326	0.182
$-$ Jaccard($\mathbf{p}_{A \to B}, \mathbf{p}_{B \to C}$)	0.226	0.29	0.184
$-$ Inter-citation ratio	0.23	0.318	0.18
$- C_A$.idf	0.248	0.478	0.168
$- C_B$.idf	0.216	0.258	0.19
$- C_C$.idf	0.22	0.256	0.194
$-$ r1.seen	0.226	0.284	0.19
$-$ r2.seen	0.228	0.298	0.184

Table 5: Ablation experiment, which removed one feature at a time from the full AdaBoost model. This experiment was performed on the development partition.

Predicted discovery	Score	Gold label
antibodies $\to$ apoptosis	1	1
apoptosis $\to$ ROS	1	1
TGF-beta $\to$ apoptosis	1	1
TLR $\to$ cascade	1	1
apoptosis $\to$ insulin	1	0
apoptosis $\to$ enzymes	1	0
antibodies $\to$ receptor	1	1
IL-6 $\to$ tumor	1	1
mutations $\to$ inflammation	0.999	1
macrophages $\to$ tumor	0.999	1

Table 6: Top 10 predicted links by the neural network model, sorted in descending order of their informativeness score.

ence and citation graphs contribute to the overall performance. Removing individual features from either group impacts performance. Several features have a high impact, including $C_{\text{inbetween}}$.avg-idf, shortest_path_length, which are extracted from the influence graph, and max $P(p_{A \to B}, p_{B \to C})$ and Jaccard($\mathbf{p}_{A \to B}, \mathbf{p}_{B \to C}$), which are extracted from the citation graph. These results demonstrate that the task of scientific discovery requires a multi-faceted approach that analyzes several graphs, including graphs that model the content of publications (our IG), as well as citation graphs.

Lastly, we rank the discoveries made by the proposed approach using the NN model, using a scoring function that combines the classifier confidence and redundancy (i.e., how many times we saw $A \to C$ with different intermediate nodes B) using a Noisy-Or formula:

$$Score(A \to C) = (1 - \prod_B (1 - prob(A \to C|B)))$$

where B loops overall intermediate nodes that support the predicted relation, and $prob(A \to C|B)$ is the classifier's output probability given one intermediate node B.[5] Table 6 lists the top 10 prediction of our approach under this scoring function. 80% of these predictions are correct (i.e., they are discovered after time $t = 2012$). Additionally, the table shows that the predictions are indeed informative: they capture fragments of protein signaling pathways, and links to biological processes (e.g., apoptosis). A few predicted links such as "TLR $\to$ cascade" are not informative, but this could be attributed to limitations in the machine reader, which failed to capture meaningful content from the destination concept ("cascade").

5 Conclusion

We proposed a novel strategy for the identification of white spaces in scientific knowledge, which are topics that are insufficiently studied and may hide important scientific discoveries. We addressed this task with a link prediction method that operates over two graphs: a graph of influence relations that were automatically extracted from over 100K papers on children's health using a machine reading tool, and which summarize the scientific knowledge in this domain, and a graph of citations originating from these papers. Using a backtesting methodology, we showed that our method is capable of predicting which influence links will be discovered in the future with a F1 score of 27 points, and a mean average precision of 68%. An ablation analysis experiment demonstrated that features extracted from both graphs contribute to overall performance. We believe this work is relevant to many actors involved in scientific discovery including researchers and program managers.

Acknowledgements

Marco Valenzuela-Escárcega, Gus Hahn-Powell, and Mihai Surdeanu declare a financial interest in lum.ai. This interest has been properly disclosed to the University of Arizona Institutional Review Committee and is managed in accordance with its conflict of interest policies. This work was funded by the Bill and Melinda Gates Foundation HBGDki Initiative.

---

[5]This ranking function was also used to generate the ranked evaluation in Table 4.

References

Michele Banko, Michael J Cafarella, Stephen Soderland, Matthew Broadhead, and Oren Etzioni. 2007. Open information extraction from the web. In IJCAI, volume 7, pages 2670–2676.

Delroy Huborn Cameron. 2014. A context-driven subgraph model for literature-based discovery. Ph.D. thesis, Wright State University.

Gus Hahn-Powell, Marco A Valenzuela-Escarcega, and Mihai Surdeanu. 2017. Swanson linking revisited: Accelerating literature-based discovery across domains using a conceptual influence graph. Proceedings of ACL 2017, System Demonstrations, pages 103–108.

Jure Leskovec, Daniel Huttenlocher, and Jon Kleinberg. 2010. Predicting positive and negative links in online social networks. In Proceedings of the 19th international conference on World wide web, pages 641–650. ACM.

David Liben-Nowell and Jon Kleinberg. 2007. The link-prediction problem for social networks. journal of the Association for Information Science and Technology, 58(7):1019–1031.

Hoifung Poon, Kristina Toutanova, and Chris Quirk. 2015. Distant supervision for cancer pathway extraction from text.

Yakub Sebastian, Eu-Gene Siew, and Sylvester O Orimaye. 2017. Emerging approaches in literature-based discovery: techniques and performance review. The Knowledge Engineering Review, 32.

Don R Swanson. 1986. Undiscovered public knowledge. The Library Quarterly, 56(2):103–118.

Marco A. Valenzuela-Escarcega, Ozgun Babur, Gus Hahn-Powell, Dane Bell, Thomas Hicks, Enrique Noriega-Atala, Xia Wang, Mihai Surdeanu, Emek Demir, and Clayton T. Morrison. 2017. Large-scale automated reading with Reach discovers new cancer driving mechanisms. In Proceedings of the Sixth BioCreative Challenge Evaluation Workshop, pages 201–203.

Jaewon Yang, Julian McAuley, and Jure Leskovec. 2014. Detecting cohesive and 2-mode communities indirected and undirected networks. In Proceedings of the 7th ACM international conference on Web search and data mining, pages 323–332. ACM.

Efficient Generation and Processing of Word Co-occurrence Networks Using corpus2graph

Zheng Zhang
LIMSI, CNRS,
Université Paris-Saclay
Orsay, France
LRI, Univ. Paris-Sud, CNRS,
Université Paris-Saclay
Orsay, France
`zheng.zhang@limsi.fr`

Ruiqing Yin
LIMSI, CNRS,
Université Paris-Saclay
Orsay, France
`ruiqing.yin@limsi.fr`

Pierre Zweigenbaum
LIMSI, CNRS,
Université Paris-Saclay
Orsay, France
`pz@limsi.fr`

Abstract

Corpus2graph is an open-source NLP-application-oriented Python package that generates a word co-occurrence network from a large corpus. It not only contains different built-in methods to preprocess words, analyze sentences, extract word pairs and define edge weights, but also supports user-customized functions. By using parallelization techniques, it can generate a large word co-occurrence network of the whole English Wikipedia data within hours. And thanks to its nodes-edges-weight three-level progressive calculation design, rebuilding networks with different configurations is even faster as it does not need to start all over again. This tool also works with other graph libraries such as igraph, NetworkX and graph-tool as a front end providing data to boost network generation speed.

1 Introduction

Word co-occurrence networks are widely used in graph-based natural language processing methods and applications, such as keyword extraction (Mihalcea and Tarau, 2004) and word sense discrimination (Ferret, 2004).

A word co-occurrence network is a graph of word interactions representing the co-occurrence of words in a corpus. An edge can be created when two words co-occur within a sentence; these words are possibly non-adjacent, with a maximum distance (in number of words, see Section 2.2) defined by a parameter d_{max} (Cancho and Solé, 2001). In an alternate definition, an edge can be created when two words co-occur in a fixed-sized sliding window moving along the entire document or sentences (Rousseau and Vazirgiannis, 2013). Despite different methods of forming edges, the structure of the network for sentences will be the same for the two above definitions if the maximum distance of the former is equal to the sliding window size of the latter. Edges can be weighted or not. An edge's weight indicates the strength of the connection between two words, which is often related to their number of co-occurrences and/or their distance in the text. Edges can be directed or undirected (Mihalcea and Radev, 2011).

While there already exist network analysis packages such as NetworkX (Hagberg et al., 2008), igraph (Csardi and Nepusz, 2006) and graph-tool (Peixoto, 2014), they do not include components to make them applicable to texts directly: users have to provide their own word preprocessor, sentence analyzer, weight function. Moreover, for certain graph-based NLP applications, it is not straightforward to find the best network configurations, e.g. the maximum distance between words. A huge number of experiments with different network configurations is inevitable, typically rebuilding the network from scratch for each new configuration. It is easy to build a word co-occurrence network from texts by using tools like textexture[1] or GoWvis[2]. But they mainly focus on network visualization and cannot handle large corpora such as the English Wikipedia.

Our contributions: To address these inconveniences of generating a word co-occurrence network from a large corpus for NLP applications, we propose corpus2graph, an open-source[3] NLP-oriented Python package designed to handle Wikipedia-level large corpora. Corpus2graph supports many language processing configurations, from word preprocessing to sentence analysis, and different ways of defining network edges and edge attributes. By using our node-edge-weight three-level progressive calculation design, it can quickly build networks for multiple configurations.

---

[1] http://textexture.com
[2] https://safetyapp.shinyapps.io/GoWvis/
[3] available at https://github.com/zzcoolj/corpus2graph

7

Proceedings of the Twelfth Workshop on Graph-Based Methods for Natural Language Processing (TextGraphs-12), pages 7–11
New Orleans, Louisiana, June 6, 2018. ©2018 Association for Computational Linguistics

We are currently using it to experiment with injecting pre-computed word co-occurrence networks into word2vec word embedding computation.

2 Efficient NLP-oriented graph generation

Our tool builds a word co-occurrence network given a source corpus and a maximal distance d_{max}. It contains three major parts: word processing, sentence analysis and word pair analysis from an NLP point of view. They correspond to three different stages in network construction.

2.1 Node level: word preprocessing

The contents of large corpora such as the whole English Wikipedia are often stored in thousands of files, where each file may contain several Wikipedia articles. To process a corpus, we consider a file as the minimal processing unit. We go through all the files in a multiprocessing way: Files are equally distributed to all processors and each processor handles one file at a time.

To reduce space requirements, we encode each file by replacing words with numeric ids. Besides, to enable independent, parallel processing of each file, these numeric ids are local to each process, hence to each file. A local-id-encoded file and its corresponding local dictionary (word → local id) are created after this process. As this process focuses on words, our tool provides several word preprocessing options such as tokenizer selection, stemmer selection, removing numbers and removing punctuation marks. It also supports user-provided word preprocessing functions.

All these local-id-encoded files and corresponding local dictionaries are stored in a specific folder (`dicts_and_encoded_texts`). Once all source files are processed, a global dictionary (word → global id) is created by merging all local dictionaries. Note that at this point, files are still encoded with local word ids.

2.2 Node co-occurrences: sentence analysis

To prepare the construction of network edges, this step aims to enumerate word co-occurrences, taking into account word distance. Given two words w_1^i and w_2^j that co-occur within a sentence at positions i and j ($i, j \in \{1 \dots l\}$ where l is the number of words in the sentence), we define their distance $d(w_1^i, w_2^j) = j - i$. For each input

δ	Word Pairs
2	(8746, 2357), (2357, 2669), (2669, 4), (4, 309), (309, 1285), (1285, 7360)
3	(8746, 2669), (2357, 4), (2669, 309), (4, 1285), (309, 7360)
4	(8746, 4), (2357, 309), (2669, 1285), (4, 7360)
5	(8746, 309), (2357, 1285), (2669, 7360)

Table 1: Word pairs for different values of distance δ in sentence "8746 2357 2669 4 309 1285 7360"

file, d_{max} output files will be created to enumerate co-occurrences: one for each distance $\delta \in \{1, \dots d_{max}\}$. They are stored in the `cooc` folder.

To prepare the aggregation of individual statistics into global statistics (see Section 2.3), each process converts local word ids into global word ids through the combination of its local dictionary and of the global dictionary. Note that at this point the global dictionary must be loaded into RAM.

Then, a sentence analyzer goes through this file sentence by sentence to extract all word co-occurrences with distances $\delta \leq d_{max}$. For instance, sentence "The NLP history started in the 1950s." may be encoded as "8746 2357 2669 4 309 1285 7360"; the sentence analyzer will extract word pairs from distance 1 to d_{max}. The results for $d_{max} = 5$ are shown in Table 1.

User-customized sentence analyzer and distance computation are also supported so that more sophisticated definitions of word pair distance can be introduced. For instance, we plan to provide a syntactic distance: the sentence analyzer will build a parse tree for each sentence and compute word pair distance as their distance in the parse tree.

Besides, in this step, we also provide an option to count the number of occurrences of each word $occ(w)$. Given that a large corpus like Wikipedia has a huge number of tokens, a global word count is convenient to enable the user to select words based on a frequency threshold before network generation. We return to this point in the next subsection.

2.3 Edge attribute level: word pair analysis

A word pair (w_1, w_2) is represented by an edge linking two nodes in the word co-occurrence network. In this step, we enrich edge information with *direction* and *weight* by word pair analysis.

Let $cooc(\delta, w_1, w_2)$ the number of co-occurrences of w_1 and w_2 with a distance of δ (Eq. 1). We define the weight $w(d_{max}, w_1, w_2)$ of an edge (w_1, w_2) as the total number of co-occurrences of w_1 and w_2 with distances $\delta \leq d_{max}$ (Eq. 2).

$$cooc(\delta, w_1, w_2) = |\{(w_1^i, w_2^j); d(w_1^i, w_2^j) = \delta\}| \quad (1)$$

$$w(d_{max}, w_1, w_2) = \sum_{\delta \leq d_{max}} cooc(\delta, w_1, w_2) \quad (2)$$

For efficiency we use an iterative algorithm (Eq. 3):

$$w(d, w_1, w_2) = \begin{cases} cooc(1, w_1, w_2), & \text{if } d = 1 \\ cooc(d, w_1, w_2) + \\ w(d-1, w_1, w_2), & \text{otherwise} \end{cases} \quad (3)$$

We calculate the edge weight of different window sizes in a stepwise fashion by applying Eq. 3. For the initial calculation, we start by counting and merging all word pair files of distance 1 in the `edges` folder generated by step 2 to get a co-occurrence count file. This file contains information on all distinct word pair co-occurrence counts for distance 1. We then follow the same principle to obtain a co-occurrence count file for distance 2. We merge this result with the previous one to get word pair co-occurrence counts for window size 2. We continue this way until distance d_{max}.

If we wish to make further experiments with a larger distance, there is no need to recompute counts from the very beginning: we just need to pick up the word pair co-occurrences of the largest distance that we already calculated and start from there. All co-occurrence count files for the different distances are stored in the `graph` folder.

Defining the weight as the sum of co-occurrences of two words with different distances is just one of the most common ways used in graph-based natural language processing applications. We also support other (built-in and user-defined) definitions of the weight. For instance, when calculating the sum of co-occurrences, we can assign different weights to co-occurrences according to the word pair distance, to make the resulting edge weight more sensitive to the word pair distance information.

For a large corpus, we may not need all edges to generate the final network. Based on the word count information from Section 2.2, we may select those nodes whose total frequency is greater than or equal to *min_count*, or the most frequent *vocab_size* number of nodes, or apply both of these constraints, before building edges and computing their weights.

3 Efficient graph processing

3.1 Matrix-type representations

Although our tool works with graph libraries like igraph, NetworkX and graph-tool as a front end, we also provide our own version of graph processing class for efficiency reasons: Most graph libraries treat graph processing problems in a network way. Their algorithms are mainly based on network concepts such as node, edge, weight, degree. Sometimes, using these concepts directly in network algorithms is intuitive but not computationally efficient. As networks and matrices are interchangeable, our graph processing class uses matrix-type representations and tries to adapt network algorithms in a matrix calculation fashion, which boosts up the calculation speed.

In our matrix representation for graph information, nodes, edges and weights are stored in an adjacency matrix A: a square matrix of dimension $|N| \times |N|$, where N is the number of nodes in the graph. Each row of this matrix stands for a starting node, each column represents one ending node and each cell contains the weight of the edge from that starting node to the ending node.

Note that not all network algorithms are suitable for adapting into a matrix version. For this reason, our graph processing class does not aim to be a replacement of the graph libraries we mentioned before. It is just a supplement, which provides matrix-based calculation versions for some of the algorithms.

To give the reader an intuition about the difference between the common network-type representation and the matrix-type representation, the coming subsection uses the random walk algorithm as an example.

3.2 Random walk

Random walks (Aldous and Fill, 2002) are widely used in graph-based natural language processing tasks, for instance word-sense disambiguation (Moro et al., 2014) and text summarization (Erkan and Radev, 2004; Zhu et al., 2007). The core of the random walk related algorithms calculation is the transition matrix P.

In the random walk scenario, starting from an initial vertex u, we cross an edge attached to u that leads to another vertex, say v (v can be u itself when there exists an edge that leads from u to u, which we call a self-loop). Element P_{uv} of the transition matrix P represents the transition probability $P(u, v)$ of the walk from vertex u to vertex v in one step. For a weighted directed network, $P(u, v)$ can be calculated as the ratio of the weight of the edge (u, v) over the sum of the weights of the edges that start from vertex u.

NetworkX (version 2.0) provides a built-in method *stochastic_graph* to calculate the transition matrix P. For directed graphs, it starts by calculating the sum of the adjacent edge weights of each node in the graph and stores all the results in memory for future usage. Then it traverses every edge (u, v), dividing its weight by the sum of the weights of the edges that start from u.

Based on the adjacency matrix A introduced in Section 3.1, the transition probability $P(u, v)$ can be expressed as:

$$P(u, v) = A_{uv} / \sum_{i=1}^{|A_u|} A_{ui}$$

The transition matrix P can be easily calculated in two steps: First, getting sums of all elements along each row and broadcasting the results against the input matrix to preserve the dimensions (*keepdims* is set to True); Second, performing element-wise division to get the ratios of each cell value to the sum of all its row's cell values. By using NumPy (Walt et al., 2011), the calculation is more efficient both in speed and memory. Besides, as the calculations are independent of each row, we can take advantage of multiprocessing to further enhance the computing speed.

4 Experiments

4.1 Set-up

In the first experiment, we generated a word co-occurrence network for a small corpus of 7416 tokens (one file of the English Wikipedia dump from April 2017) without using multiprocessing on a computer equipped with the Intel Core i7-6700HQ processor. Our tool serves as a front end to provide nodes and edges to the graph libraries NetworkX, igraph and graph-tool. In contrast, the baseline method processes the corpus sentence by sentence, extracting word pairs with a distance $\delta \leq d_{max}$ and adding them to the graph as edges (or updating the weight of edges) through these libraries. All distinct tokens in this corpus are considered as nodes.

In the second experiment, we used our tool to extract nodes and edges for the generation of a word co-occurrence network on the entire English Wikipedia dump from April 2017 using 50 logical cores on a server with 4 Intel Xeon E5-4620 processors , $d_{max} = 5$, *min_count* $= 5$ and *vocab_size* $= 10000$.

In the last experiment, we compared the random walk transition matrix calculation speed on the word co-occurrence network built from the previous experiment result between our method and the built-in method of NetworkX (version 2.0) on a computer equipped with Intel Core i7-6700HQ processor.

4.2 Results

	NetworkX	igraph	graph-tool
baseline	**4.88**	8727.49	77.70
corpus2graph	15.90	**14.47**	**14.31**

Table 2: Word network generation speed (seconds)

Table 2 shows that regardless of the library used to receive graph information generated by corpus2graph, it takes around 15 seconds from the small Wikipedia corpora to the final word co-occurrence network. And our method performs much better than the baseline method with igraph and graph-tool even without using multiprocessing. We found that in general loading all edges and nodes information at once is faster than loading edge and node information one by one and it takes approximately the same time for all graph libraries. As for NetworkX, the baseline method is faster. But as the corpora get larger, the baseline model uses more and more memory to store the continuously growing graph, and the processing time increases too.

For the second experiment, our tool took around 236 seconds for node processing (Section 2.1), 2501 seconds for node co-occurrence analysis (Section 2.2) and 8004 seconds for edge information enriching (Section 2.3). In total, it took less than 3 hours to obtain all the nodes and weighted edges for the subsequent network generation.

Generation of:	network	transition matrix
NetworkX	447.71	2533.88
corpus2graph	**116.15**	**1.06**

Table 3: Transition matrix calculation speed (seconds)

Table 3 shows the results of the third experiment. Loading network information into our graph processing class is faster than loading into the graph class of NetworkX. Moreover, our random walk transition matrix calculation method is 2390 times faster than the built-in method in NetworkX.

5 Conclusion

We presented in this paper an NLP-application-oriented Python package that generates a word co-occurrence network from a large corpus. Experiments show that our tool can boost network generation and graph processing speed compared to baselines.

Possible extensions of this work would be to support more graph processing methods and to connect our tool to more existing graph libraries.

References

David Aldous and James Allen Fill. 2002. Reversible Markov chains and random walks on graphs. Unfinished monograph, recompiled 2014, available at http://www.stat.berkeley.edu/~aldous/RWG/book.html.

Ramon Ferrer i Cancho and Richard V. Solé. 2001. The small world of human language. *Proceedings of the Royal Society of London B: Biological Sciences*, 268(1482):2261–2265.

Gabor Csardi and Tamas Nepusz. 2006. The igraph software package for complex network research. *InterJournal*, Complex Systems:1695.

Günes Erkan and Dragomir R Radev. 2004. Lexrank: Graph-based lexical centrality as salience in text summarization. *Journal of Artificial Intelligence Research*, 22:457–479.

Olivier Ferret. 2004. Discovering word senses from a network of lexical cooccurrences. In *Proceedings of the 20th International Conference on Computational Linguistics*, COLING '04, Stroudsburg, PA, USA. Association for Computational Linguistics.

Aric A. Hagberg, Daniel A. Schult, and Pieter J. Swart. 2008. Exploring network structure, dynamics, and function using NetworkX. In *Proceedings of the 7th Python in Science Conference (SciPy2008)*, pages 11–15, Pasadena, CA USA.

Rada Mihalcea and Paul Tarau. 2004. Textrank: Bringing order into text. In *Proceedings of the 2004 conference on empirical methods in natural language processing*.

Rada F. Mihalcea and Dragomir R. Radev. 2011. *Graph-based Natural Language Processing and Information Retrieval*, 1st edition. Cambridge University Press, New York, NY, USA.

Andrea Moro, Alessandro Raganato, and Roberto Navigli. 2014. Entity linking meets word sense disambiguation: a unified approach. *TACL*, 2:231–244.

Tiago P. Peixoto. 2014. The graph-tool python library. *figshare*.

François Rousseau and Michalis Vazirgiannis. 2013. Graph-of-word and tw-idf: New approach to ad hoc ir. In *Proceedings of the 22Nd ACM International Conference on Information & Knowledge Management*, CIKM '13, pages 59–68, New York, NY, USA. ACM.

Stefan van der Walt, S. Chris Colbert, and Gael Varoquaux. 2011. The numpy array: A structure for efficient numerical computation. *Computing in Science and Engg.*, 13(2):22–30.

Xiaojin Zhu, Andrew Goldberg, Jurgen Van Gael, and David Andrzejewski. 2007. Improving diversity in ranking using absorbing random walks. In *Human Language Technologies 2007: The Conference of the North American Chapter of the Association for Computational Linguistics; Proceedings of the Main Conference*, pages 97–104.

Multi-hop Inference for Sentence-level TextGraphs:
How Challenging is Meaningfully Combining Information for Science Question Answering?

Peter A. Jansen

School of Information, University of Arizona, Tucson, AZ

pajansen@email.arizona.edu

Abstract

Question Answering for complex questions is often modelled as a graph construction or traversal task, where a solver must build or traverse a graph of facts that answer and explain a given question. This "multi-hop" inference has been shown to be extremely challenging, with few models able to aggregate more than two facts before being overwhelmed by "semantic drift", or the tendency for long chains of facts to quickly drift off topic. This is a major barrier to current inference models, as even elementary science questions require an average of 4 to 6 facts to answer and explain. In this work we empirically characterize the difficulty of building or traversing a graph of sentences connected by lexical overlap, by evaluating chance sentence aggregation quality through 9,784 manually-annotated judgements across knowledge graphs built from three free-text corpora (including study guides and Simple Wikipedia). We demonstrate semantic drift tends to be high and aggregation quality low, at between 0.04% and 3%, and highlight scenarios that maximize the likelihood of meaningfully combining information.

1 Introduction

Question answering (QA) is a task where models must find answers to natural language questions, either by retrieving these answers from a corpus, or inferring them by some inference process. Retrieval methods model QA as an answer sentence selection task, where a solver must find a sentence or short continuous passage of text in a corpus that answers the question (Moschitti et al., 2007; Severyn and Moschitti, 2012, inter alia). These methods often fall short for questions requiring complex inference, such as those in the science domain, where nearly 80% of even 4th grade science exam questions require some form of causal, model-based, or otherwise com-

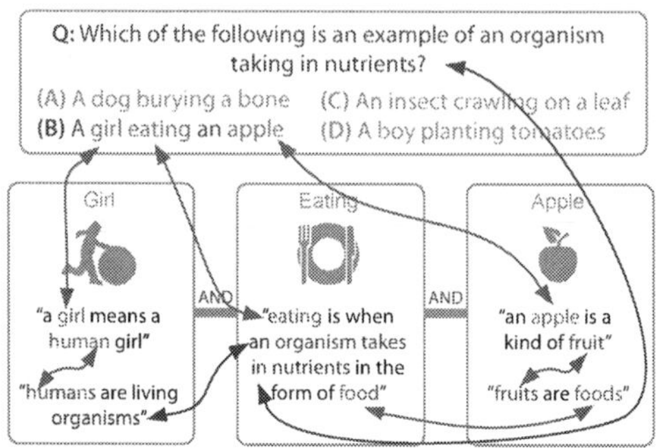

Figure 1: An example multiple choice 4th grade science question from the NY Regents exam, and a graph of 5 sentences that answer and explain the answer to this question. Edges represent lexical overlap.

plex inference to answer and explain (Clark et al., 2013; Jansen et al., 2016), and a single continuous passage of text rarely describes the reasoning required to move from question to correct answer. In these cases, *multiple sentences*, often from different parts of a text, different documents, or different knowledge bases must be aggregated together to build a complete answer and explanation.

Aggregating knowledge to support inference and complex question answering is often framed as a graph construction or traversal problem (e.g. Khashabi et al., 2016), where the solver must find paths that link sentences that contain question terms with sentences that contain answer terms through some number of intermediate sentences (see Figure 1). In these knowledge graphs, nodes represent facts or single sentences, and edges between nodes represent some signal that the facts are interrelated, such as having lexical overlap.

Information aggregation or "multi-hop" graph traversal has been shown to be extremely challenging, with QA solvers generally showing only modest performance benefits when aggregating information, and diminishing returns as the amount of aggregation increases. In the elementary sci-

Proceedings of the Twelfth Workshop on Graph-Based Methods for Natural Language Processing (TextGraphs-12), pages 12–17
New Orleans, Louisiana, June 6, 2018. ©2018 Association for Computational Linguistics

ence domain, current estimates suggest that an average of 4 to 6 sentences are required to answer and explain a given question (Jansen et al., 2016, 2018), while recent QA solvers generally struggle to meaningfully aggregate more than two free-text sentences (Jansen et al., 2017), even when using alternate representations including semi-structured tables (Khashabi et al., 2016) or graphs of words or syntactic dependencies traversed using monolingual alignment or PageRank variants in open-domain QA (Fried et al., 2015). Fried et al. (2015) suggest these performance limitations are due to *"semantic drift"*, where as the number of sentences being aggregated increases, so do the chances of making a misstep in the aggregation – for example, aggregating a sentence about *seed funding for a company* when making an inference about the *stages of plant growth*. This appears to occur across a variety of solvers, representations, and methods for aggregation, and is leading to both the development of datasets specifically designed for multi-hop QA (Jansen et al., 2016, 2018; Welbl et al., 2017), as well as methods of controlling for semantic drift in knowledge graphs constructed from (for example) OpenIE triples using either support graphs (Khot et al., 2017) or drift-sensitive random walks (Kwon et al., 2018).

In an effort to better understand the challenges of inference and explanation construction for QA, here we characterize the difficulty of the information aggregation task in the context of science exams. The contributions of this work are:

1. We provide the first empirical characterization of the difficulty of information aggregation by manually evaluating sentence aggregation quality using 9,784 annotated judgements across 14 representative exam questions, highlighting specific patterns of lexical overlap between question, answer, and candidate sentence that maximize the chances of successful aggregation.

2. We evaluate aggregation difficulty across three knowledge resources, and empirically demonstrate that while moving to open domain resources increases knowledge coverage, it also increases the difficulty of the information aggregation task by more than an order of magnitude.

3. We evaluate aggregating up to three sentences that connect terms in the question to terms in the answer, and show that this suffers both from sparsity (even on Wikipedia-scale corpora), as well as a very low probability of producing meaningful aggregations (0.04% to 3%) through lexical overlap alone.

2 Approach

Questions: Due to the magnitude of manual annotation, we drew 14 representative questions annotated as likely requiring inference[1] from the 432 training questions in the AI2 Open Elementary Science Questions set[2], originally drawn from standardized science exams in 12 US states. Questions span 14 common curriculum topics, including changes of state, planetary motion, environmental adaptations, the life cycle, inherited traits, magnetism, and measurement. For context, to date, the best-performing systems report answering just under 60% of elementary science questions correctly (Jauhar et al., 2016).

2.1 Corpora

We generate and evaluate three separate graphs constructed from three independent corpora:

Science Explanations Corpus: An explanation corpus of 1,364 sentences from Jansen et al. (2016) designed to construct high-quality explanations for the AI2 question set through aggregation.

Study Guide Corpus: An in-domain corpus of 2,503 sentences from two study guides for the New York and Virginia standardized exams.

Simple Wikipedia: A large open-domain corpus of 848,920 sentences retrieved from Simple Wikipedia and included in the AristoMini corpus[2].

2.2 Methods

Here we simulate the graph-based inference process by creating short chains of sentences interconnected based on shared words between those sentences. Specifically, two sentences are said to be connected if they share at least one content lemma *(noun, verb, or adjective)* in common. Sentences with the same lemma but different parts of speech are not connected (e.g. a sentence containing *plant_VB* is not connected to a sentence containing *plant_NN*). Lemmatization and part-of-speech tagging are provided by the Stanford CoreNLP toolkit (Manning et al., 2014).

---

[1] Our results did not substantially change when data from only half the questions were used, suggesting the aggregate statistics from the 9,784 manual judgements are stable.

[2] `http://allenai.org/data.html`

Q: What is the main purpose of the flowers of a peach tree?
A: to attract bees for pollination.

Example Ratings:
High: The flower helps the plant reproduce because it contains the pollen and eggs.
Possible: Seeds grow in the center of a flower and continue to develop there after the petals fall off the plant.
Topical/Unlikely: There are four major parts of a plant: roots, stem, leaves, and flower.
Offtopic: The average life span of a worker bee is 1 year.

Table 1: Example ratings on a 4-point rating scale describing the perceived utility of each sentence towards an explanation for why the answer is correct (high, possible, topical, offtopic). Sentences are from the Study Guide corpus, and each have lexical overlap with the question and/or answer.

For a given question, sentences in one corpus are identified that have lexical overlap with either the question terms, answer terms, or both question and answer terms. We then manually rate the relevance of each sentence on a 4-point scale using the following criterion: *"What is the likelihood that this knowledge would contribute to an explanation for why the answer is correct?"*. Example ratings are included in Table 1.

2.3 Connectivity Characterization

Here, we denote the question text as Q, the correct answer text as A, and a sentence from the corpus with overlapping terms as S_x, where x is either Q or A. We characterize the utility of sentences towards building an explanation in five scenarios:

Direct lexical overlap:

1. $Q \leftrightarrow S_Q$: Sentences that have lexical overlap with the question.

2. $S_A \leftrightarrow A$: Sentences that have lexical overlap with the answer.

3. $Q \leftrightarrow S_{QA} \leftrightarrow A$: Sentences that have lexical overlap with both question and answer.

Indirect (aggregating) overlap:

4. $Q \leftrightarrow S_Q \leftrightarrow S_A \leftrightarrow A$: Aggregating two sentences that individually have lexical overlap with the question or answer, and that also have lexical overlap with each other.

5. $Q \leftrightarrow S_Q \leftrightarrow S_O \leftrightarrow S_A \leftrightarrow A$: Aggregating three sentences: two sentences that individually have lexical overlap with the question or answer, and that are connected by a third sentence S_O that has lexical overlap with both S_Q and S_A, but not with Q or A.

3   Results and Discussion

What proportion of sentences with direct lexical overlap to the question and answer contain highly relevant information? The results of the direct characterization are shown in Table 2. The overall proportion of corpus sentences containing relevant information to the question are low, with 5.5% of sentences rated as highly useful in the explanation corpus, 1.7% in the Study Guide corpus, and only 0.1% in the large Simple Wikipedia corpus. Sentence utility increases as the lexical overlap (number of terms matched) increases. Similarly, sentences with terms from the answer are *3 to 5* times more likely to be highly relevant than sentences with question terms. Sentences that overlap on both question and answer terms have a substantially increased probability of being rated highly relevant compared to sentences with a single question or answer term (e.g. 21.4% vs 1.7% and 5.2%, respectively, for the Study Guide corpus), but are sparse, occurring an average of approximately once per question.

When aggregating two sentences, what proportion will contain highly relevant information? The probability of aggregating two sentences that individually lexically overlap with the question or answer, and also lexically overlap with each other, $Q \leftrightarrow S_Q \leftrightarrow S_A \leftrightarrow A$, is shown in Table 3. The likelihood of aggregating two sentences from the Study Guide corpus that were both highly rated and that lexically overlap by at least one term is 3.0%, and when expanding this to allow for aggregating sentences with high or possible ratings *(bolded square)*, this likelihood increases to 6.6%. For the Simple Wikipedia corpus these probabilities are one to two orders of magnitude lower, at 0.04% and 0.3%, respectively.

When restricting 2-sentence aggregations to cases of moderate lexical overlap, where $S_Q \leftrightarrow S_A$ overlap by *2 or more lemmas* not found in the question or answer, quality improves substantially

---

[3]The scale of the Simple Wikipedia corpus makes manual evaluation intractable. Here we subsample to rate 50 sentences with each pattern of lexical overlap, and limit our analysis to 7 questions. For example, for the question in in Table 1, we rate 50 sentences that have lexical overlap only with the word *flowers_NN*, another 50 that overlap with *flowers_NN* and *purpose_NN*, and so on. In practice, due to the relative sparsity of multiword matches, *we evaluate nearly all cases where the lexical overlap consists of two or more words*, and the subsampling only affects estimates of single overlapping lemma matches for this corpus *(leftmost columns in table)*.

	1 overlapping lemma			2 overlapping lemmas			3+ overlapping lemmas		
	S_Q	S_A	S_{QA}	S_Q	S_A	S_{QA}	S_Q	S_A	S_{QA}
Explanation Corpus (1,364 sentences)									
Highly likely	5.5%	18.4%	-	18.2%	66.7%	65.6%	40.0%	-	100%
Possible	4.8%	8.5%	-	22.7%	6.7%	9.4%	40.0%	-	0%
Topical	14.1%	26.9%	-	18.2%	0%	18.8%	0%	-	0%
Off topic	75.5%	46.2%	-	40.9%	26.7%	6.3%	20.0%	-	0%
N (Samples)	992	223	-	44	15	32	5	0	7
Study Guide Corpus (2,503 sentences)									
Highly likely	1.7%	5.2%	-	6.6%	55.6%	21.4%	27.8%	-	58.8%
Possible	2.1%	6.3%	-	12.4%	5.6%	12.5%	27.8%	-	17.6%
Topical	6.7%	9.6%	-	24.1%	16.7%	12.5%	11.1%	-	5.9%
Off topic	89.6%	79.0%	-	56.9%	22.2%	53.6%	33.3%	-	17.6%
N (Samples)	2133	480	-	137	18	56	18	0	17
Simple Wikipedia Corpus (848,920 sentences, subsampled[3])									
Highly likely	0.1%	0.5%	-	0.4%	11.2%	1.7%	0.6%	50.0%	16.1%
Possible	0.2%	1.1%	-	1.8%	6.7%	3.3%	2.5%	50.0%	19.4%
Topical	0.8%	3.4%	-	3.4%	17.9%	8.2%	5.0%	0.0%	14.5%
Off topic	98.9%	95.0%	-	94.4%	64.2%	86.8%	91.9%	0.0%	50.0%
N (Samples)	2102	880	-	1399	134	599	161	2	62

Table 2: Observed frequencies for sentences with given utility ratings for the three categories of direct (lexical overlap) connections: $Q \leftrightarrow S_Q$, $S_A \leftrightarrow A$, and $Q \leftrightarrow S_{QA} \leftrightarrow A$, and various degrees of lexical overlap.

Explanation Corpus (1,979 samples)

		S_A Rating			
		Highly	*Possible*	*Topical*	*OffTopic*
S_Q Rating	*Highly*	**13.4%**	**3.8%**	3.4%	1.1%
	Possible	**3.4%**	**0.4%**	1.1%	0.6%
	Topical	7.5%	1.3%	8.0%	4.5%
	Offtopic	16.3%	11.0%	9.1%	14.9%

Study Guide Corpus (8,096 samples)

		S_A Rating			
		Highly	*Possible*	*Topical*	*OffTopic*
S_Q Rating	*Highly*	**3.0%**	**0.7%**	0.7%	1.3%
	Possible	**2.1%**	**0.8%**	0.8%	1.2%
	Topical	3.8%	2.0%	2.7%	4.4%
	Offtopic	17.0%	6.4%	10.9%	42.2%

Simple Wikipedia Corpus (23,750 samples)

		S_A Rating			
		Highly	*Possible*	*Topical*	*OffTopic*
S_Q Rating	*Highly*	**0.04%**	**0.04%**	0.06%	0.0%
	Possible	**0.1%**	**0.1%**	0.3%	1.7%
	Topical	0.1%	0.02%	0.2%	2.1%
	Offtopic	2.4%	2.0%	7.2%	82.9%

Table 3: Observed frequencies for aggregating two sentences together with specific utility ratings in the $Q \leftrightarrow S_Q \leftrightarrow S_A \leftrightarrow A$ condition across each corpus. Here, one sentence in the pair has overlapping terms in the question, the other sentence has overlapping terms in the answer, and both sentences lexically overlap with each other on *one or more* terms that are not found in either the question or answer. Axes represent the individual (nonaggregated) ratings of each sentence (Q or A). The bolded square represents the proportion of lexically connected sentence pairs where utility ratings for both sentences are either *high* or *possible*.

on the Study Guide corpus, with 12.5% of these aggregates containing sentences both rated *highly relevant* (N=1,262), or an average of 11 per question. The pattern is similar for the Explanation and SimpleWiki corpora, but scaled up by a factor of 2-4, and down by a factor of 10-40, respectively.[4]

When aggregating three sentences, what proportion of intermediate sentences are highly relevant? To characterize the number of possible 3-sentence aggregations of the form $Q \leftrightarrow S_Q \leftrightarrow S_O \leftrightarrow S_A \leftrightarrow A$, with each sentence rated as having a *highly relevant* or *possible* utility for explanations, we retrieved all intermediate sentences S_O in the corpus such that (a) S_O contains overlapping lemmas with both S_Q and S_A that are not found in the question or answer, and (b) both S_Q and S_A have ratings of either *highly relevant* or *possible*. The overall number of intermediate sentences meeting this criterion was small (17 for the Study Guide corpus across all 14 questions, and 251 for the Simple Wikipedia corpus). We manually rated these intermediate sentences, finding a small proportion had favourable utility ratings, with 1.5% receiving ratings of *highly relevant* and 2% receiving *possible*. This suggests that both sparsity and drift make aggregating three sentences highly unlikely, even in large million-sentence-scale corpora such as Simple Wikipedia.

---

[4]Due to space limitations, this table is not shown.

Overall, what is chance performance for combining information to generate real explanations? Previous work suggests that real explanations for elementary science questions require aggregating an average of 4 to 6 separate facts to answer and explain (Jansen et al., 2016, 2018), with this value ranging between 1 fact to more than a dozen facts per question, depending on the amount of question-specific knowledge and world knowledge required. Extrapolating from our empirical analysis[5] suggests that the chance of generating a 4-fact aggregation of the form $Q \leftrightarrow S_Q \leftrightarrow S_O \leftrightarrow S_O \leftrightarrow S_A \leftrightarrow A$ is likely to be extremely improbable, at approximately 1 in 187,000 for the Study Guide corpus, and 1 in 17 million with the Simple Wikipedia corpus, in the case of sentences having a single overlapping lemma. Where S_Q and S_A share two overlapping lemmas with the question, this increases to approximately 1 in 7,000 for the Study Guide corpus, and 1 in 207,000 for the Simple Wikipedia corpus, but is still improbable.

Building graphs based solely on lexical overlap captures only a fraction of the possible meaningful connections between knowledge in a corpus. How might this limitation affect this empirical analysis? Lexical overlap is a common method of building knowledge graphs for QA (e.g. Khashabi et al., 2016; Jansen et al., 2017), as two sentences having the same words has been regarded as a strong signal that they may contain mutually beneficial content for the inference task. While other methods of connection, such as Word-Net synsets to capture synonymy or word embeddings to capture associative relations, are likely to increase the recall of sentences in a corpus relevant to a given question, we hypothesize that lexical overlap – as poorly as we have shown it performs empirically – is likely a higher precision method of creating meaningful connections than these other connection methods. In this way we propose lexical overlap can be viewed as a baseline for other knowledge graph connection methodologies to be evaluated against.

Evaluating the proportion of meaningful connections in graphs built from specific knowledge resources provides only a partial understanding of the challenges of information aggregation, because it doesn't capture how well specific inference methods may perform on a given knowledge graph. A central limitation of this empirical evaluation is that it evaluates the probability of meaningfully assembling knowledge in three specific knowledge resources, rather than the empirical performance of specific inference algorithms on assembling knowledge towards the QA and explanation construction task with these specific resources. Combining information to form inferences is one of the central challenges in contemporary question answering, and few models appear able to consistently aggregate more than two facts in support of this inference task. While a variety of different methods of information aggregation have been proposed, our ultimate evaluation metric for many of these models has been the overall proportion of questions answered correctly, rather than a targeted evaluation of the information aggregation mechanism. Methods such as evaluating inference performance as the number of aggregation steps increases (e.g. Fried et al., 2015; Jansen et al., 2017) begin to provide insight on the efficacy of specific methods of information aggregation, but these methods must be paired with a knowledge graph with known connectivity properties to provide a detailed characterization of the performance of specific aggregation methods on the information aggregation task.

4   Conclusion

We empirically demonstrate that aggregating multiple sentences together to support inference for QA is extremely challenging. For the in-domain study guide corpus, only 3% of 2-sentence $Q \leftrightarrow S_Q \leftrightarrow S_A \leftrightarrow A$ aggregations were rated as highly useful, while this falls to 0.04% for the open domain corpus. In spite of the size of Simple Wikipedia, 3-sentence aggregations are sparse, and substantially reduce the chance of meaningfully aggregating sentences to the point of improbability. Taken together, our analysis suggests the ability to generate inferences incorporating *4 to 6 facts* required for the average question is unlikely without high-precision means of concept matching beyond lexical overlap, and methods of controlling for drift, or reducing drift through pairing with close-domain corpora. Our ratings for the open Explanation and Simple Wikipedia corpora are available at http://cognitiveai.org/explanationbank/.

---

[5] This extrapolation uses the empirically derived probability of a meaningful S_O transition to be 3.5% (1.5% *highly* + 2.0% *possible*). Similarly, probabilities for S_Q and S_A add both *highly* and *possible* transition probabilities from Table 2.

References

Peter Clark, Philip Harrison, and Niranjan Balasubramanian. 2013. A study of the knowledge base requirements for passing an elementary science test. In *Proceedings of the 2013 Workshop on Automated Knowledge Base Construction*, AKBC'13, pages 37–42.

Daniel Fried, Peter Jansen, Gustave Hahn-Powell, Mihai Surdeanu, and Peter Clark. 2015. Higher-order lexical semantic models for non-factoid answer reranking. *Transactions of the Association for Computational Linguistics*, 3:197–210.

Peter Jansen, Niranjan Balasubramanian, Mihai Surdeanu, and Peter Clark. 2016. What's in an explanation? characterizing knowledge and inference requirements for elementary science exams. In *Proceedings of COLING 2016, the 26th International Conference on Computational Linguistics: Technical Papers*, pages 2956–2965, Osaka, Japan. The COLING 2016 Organizing Committee.

Peter Jansen, Rebecca Sharp, Mihai Surdeanu, and Peter Clark. 2017. Framing qa as building and ranking intersentence answer justifications. *Computational Linguistics*.

Peter Jansen, Elizabeth Wainwright, Steven Marmorstein, and Clayton T. Morrison. 2018. Worldtree: A corpus of explanation graphs for elementary science questions supporting multi-hop inference. In *Proceedings of the 11th International Conference on Language Resources and Evaluation (LREC)*.

Sujay Kumar Jauhar, Peter D Turney, and Eduard H Hovy. 2016. Tables as semi-structured knowledge for question answering. In *Proceedings of the 54th Annual Meeting of the Association for Computational Linguistics (ACL)*.

Daniel Khashabi, Tushar Khot, Ashish Sabharwal, Peter Clark, Oren Etzioni, and Dan Roth. 2016. Question answering via integer programming over semi-structured knowledge. In *Proceedings of the International Joint Conference on Artificial Intelligence*, IJCAI'16, pages 1145–1152.

Tushar Khot, Ashish Sabharwal, and Peter Clark. 2017. Answering complex questions using open information extraction. In *Proceedings of the 55th Annual Meeting of the Association for Computational Linguistics, ACL 2017, Vancouver, Canada, July 30 - August 4, Volume 2: Short Papers*, pages 311–316.

Heeyoung Kwon, Harsh Trivedi, Peter Jansen, Mihai Surdeanu, and Niranjan Balasubramanian. 2018. Controlling information aggregation for complex question answering. In *Proceedings of the 40th European Conference on Information Retrieval (ECIR)*.

Christopher D Manning, Mihai Surdeanu, John Bauer, Jenny Finkel, Steven J Bethard, and David McClosky. 2014. The stanford corenlp natural language processing toolkit. In *Proceedings of 52nd Annual Meeting of the Association for Computational Linguistics: System Demonstrations*, pages 55–60.

Alessandro Moschitti, Silvia Quarteroni, Roberto Basili, and Suresh Manandhar. 2007. Exploiting syntactic and shallow semantic kernels for question/answer classification. In *Proceedings of the 45th Annual Meeting of the Association for Computational Linguistics (ACL)*, pages 776–783, Prague, Czech Republic.

Aliaksei Severyn and Alessandro Moschitti. 2012. Structural relationships for large-scale learning of answer re-ranking. In *SIGIR*.

Johannes Welbl, Pontus Stenetorp, and Sebastian Riedel. 2017. Constructing datasets for multi-hop reading comprehension across documents. *arXiv preprint arXiv:1710.06481*.

Multi-Sentence Compression with Word Vertex-Labeled Graphs and Integer Linear Programming

Elvys Linhares Pontes[1], Stéphane Huet[1], Thiago Gouveia da Silva[1,3,4]
and **Juan-Manuel Torres-Moreno[1,2]**

1 - LIA, Université d'Avignon et des Pays de Vaucluse, Avignon, France
2 - École Polytechnique de Montréal, Montréal, Canada
3 - Inst. de Computação – Univ. Federal Fluminense (UFF), Niterói – RJ – Brazil
4 - Inst. Federal de Educação, Ciência e Tecnologia da Paraíba (IFPB), PB – Brazil
elvys.linhares-pontes@alumni.univ-avignon.fr
stephane.huet@univ-avignon.fr
thiago.gouveia@ifpb.edu.br
juan-manuel.torres@univ-avignon.fr

Andréa C. Linhares
Universidade Federal do Ceará, Sobral, Brazil
andrea@sobral.ufc.br

Abstract

Multi-Sentence Compression (MSC) aims to generate a short sentence with key information from a cluster of closely related sentences. MSC enables summarization and question-answering systems to generate outputs combining fully formed sentences from one or several documents. This paper describes a new Integer Linear Programming method for MSC using a vertex-labeled graph to select different keywords, and novel 3-grams scores to generate more informative sentences while maintaining their grammaticality. Our system is of good quality and outperforms the state-of-the-art for evaluations led on news dataset. We led both automatic and manual evaluations to determine the informativeness and the grammaticality of compressions for each dataset. Additional tests, which take advantage of the fact that the length of compressions can be modulated, still improve ROUGE scores with shorter output sentences.

1 Introduction

The increased number of electronic devices (smartphones, tablets, etc.) have made access to information easier and faster. Websites such as Wikipedia or news aggregators can provide detailed data on various issues but texts may be long and convey a lot of information. One solution to this problem is the generation of summaries containing only key information.

Among the various applications of Natural Language Processing (NLP), Automatic Text Summarization (ATS) aims to automatically identify the relevant data inside one or more documents, and create a condensed text with the main information. Summarization systems usually rely on statistical, morphological and syntactic analysis approaches (Torres-Moreno, 2014). Some of them use Multi-Sentence Compression (MSC) in order to produce from a set of similar sentences a small-sized sentence which is both grammatically correct and informative (Filippova, 2010; Banerjee et al., 2015). Although compression is a challenging task, it is appropriate to generate summaries that are more informative than state-of-the-art extraction methods for ATS.

The contributions of this article are two-fold. (i) We present a new model for MSC that extends the common approach based on Graph Theory, using vertex-labeled graphs and Integer Linear Programming (ILP) to select the best compression. The vertex-labeled graphs are used to model a cluster of similar sentences with keywords, while the optimization criterion introduces a novel 3-grams score to enhance the correctness of sentences. (ii) We can set up a maximum length for the compression. The system can generate shorter compressions losing some information, or privilege the informativeness generating longer compressions. Evaluations led with both automatic metrics and human evaluations show that our ILP model consistently generate more informative sentences than two baselines while maintaining their grammaticality. Our approach is able to choose the amount of information to keep in the compression output, through the definition of the number of keywords

Proceedings of the Twelfth Workshop on Graph-Based Methods for Natural Language Processing (TextGraphs-12), pages 18–27
New Orleans, Louisiana, June 6, 2018. ©2018 Association for Computational Linguistics

to consider in documents.

This paper is organized as follows: we describe and survey the MSC problem in Section 2. Next, we detail our approach in Section 3. The experiments and the results are discussed in Sections 4 and 5. Lastly, we provide the Conclusion and some final comments in Section 6.

2   Related Work

Sentence Compression (SC) aims at producing a reduced grammatically correct sentence. Compressions may have different Compression Ratio (CR) levels[1], whereby the lower the CR level, the higher the reduction of the information is. SC can be employed in the contexts of the summarization of documents, the generation of article titles or the simplification of complex sentences, using diverse methods such as optimization (Clarke and Lapata, 2007, 2008), syntactic analysis, deletion of words (Filippova et al., 2015) or generation of sentences (Rush et al., 2015; Miao and Blunsom, 2016).

Multi-Sentence Compression (MSC), also coined as Multi-Sentence Fusion, is a variation of SC. Unlike SC, MSC combines the information of a cluster of similar sentences to generate a new sentence, hopefully grammatically correct, which compresses the most relevant data of this cluster. The idea of MSC was introduced by Barzilay and McKeown (2005), who developed a multi-document summarizer which represents each sentence as a dependency tree; their approach aligns and combines these trees to fusion sentences. Filippova and Strube (2008) also used dependency trees to align each cluster of related sentences and generated a new tree this time with ILP to compress the information. In 2010, Filippova presented a new model for MSC, simple but effective, which is based on Graph Theory and a list of stopwords. She used a Word Graph (WG) to represent and to compress the related sentences of the document D based on the cohesion of words. The vertices and the arcs weights of WG represent the word/POS pairs and the levels of cohesion between two words in the document (Equation 1), respectively.

$$w(i, j) = \frac{\text{cohesion}(i, j)}{\text{freq}(i) \times \text{freq}(j)}, \qquad (1)$$

---

[1]The CR is the length of the compression divided by the average length of all source sentences

$$\text{cohesion}(i, j) = \frac{\text{freq}(i) + \text{freq}(j)}{\sum_{s \in D} \text{diff}(s, i, j)^{-1}}, \qquad (2)$$

where freq(i) is the word frequency mapped to the vertex i and the function diff(s, i, j) refers to the distance between the offset positions of words i and j in the sentences s of D containing these two words. Finally, she chose as the best MSC the path with the lowest average arc weight among the 50 shortest paths (more details in (Filippova, 2010)).

Inspired by the good results of the Filippova's method, many studies have used it in a first step to generate a list of the N shortest paths, then have relied on different reranking strategies to analyze the candidates and select the best compression (Boudin and Morin, 2013; Tzouridis et al., 2014; Luong et al., 2015; Banerjee et al., 2015). Boudin and Morin (2013) developed a reranking method measuring the relevance of a candidate compression using *keyphrases*, obtained with the TextRank algorithm (Mihalcea and Tarau, 2004), and the length of the sentence. Another reranking strategy was proposed by Luong et al. (2015). Their method ranks the sentences from the counts of unigrams occurring in every source sentence. ShafieiBavani et al. (2016) also used a WG model; their approach consists of three main components: (i) a merging stage based on Multiword Expressions (MWE), (ii) a mapping strategy based on synonymy between words and (iii) a reranking step to identify the best compression candidates generated using a POS-based language model (POS-LM). Tzouridis et al. (2014) proposed a structured learning-based approach. Instead of applying heuristics as Filippova (2010), they adapted the decoding process to the data by parameterizing a shortest path algorithm. They devised a structural support vector machine to learn the shortest path in possibly high dimensional joint feature spaces and proposed a generalized, loss-augmented decoding algorithm that is solved exactly by ILP in polynomial time.

We found two other studies that applied ILP to combine and compress several sentences. Banerjee et al. (2015) developed a multi-document ATS system that generated summaries based on compression of similar sentences. They used Filippova's method to generate 200 random compressed sentences. Then they created an ILP model to select the most informative and grammatically correct compression. Thadani and McKeown (2013) proposed another ILP model using an inference approach for sentence fusion. Their ILP formulation relies on n-grams factorization and aims at avoiding cycles and disconnected structures.

Following previous studies that rely on Graph Theory with good results, this work presents a new ILP framework that takes into account keywords and 3-grams for MSC. We compare our learning approach to the graph-based sentence compression techniques proposed by Filippova (2010) and Boudin and Morin (2013), considered as state-of-the-art methods for MSC. We intend to apply our method on various languages and not to be dependent on linguistic resources or tools specific to languages. This leads us to put aside systems which, despite being competitive, rely on resources like WordNet or Multiword expression detectors (ShafieiBavani et al., 2016).

3   Our Approach

Filippova's method chooses the path in a WG with the lowest score taking into account the level of cohesion between two adjacent words in the document. However, two words with a strong cohesion do not necessarily have a good informativeness because the cohesion only measures the distance and the frequency of words in the sentences. In this work, we propose a method to concurrently analyze cohesion, keywords and 3-grams in order to generate a more informative and comprehensible compression.

Our method calculates the shortest path from the cohesion of words and grants bonuses to the paths that have different keywords and frequent 3-grams. For this purpose, our approach is based on Filippova's method to model a document D as a graph and to calculate the cohesion of words. In addition, we analyze the keywords and the *3-grams* of the document to favor hypotheses with meaningful information.

3.1   Keyword and 3-grams extraction

Introducing keywords in the graph helps the system to generate more informative compressions because it takes into account the words that are representative of the cluster to calculate the best path in the graph, and not only the cohesion and frequency of words. Keywords can be identified for each cluster with various extraction methods and we study three widely used techniques: Latent

Semantic Indexing (LSI), Latent Dirichlet Allocation (LDA) and TextRank. Despite the small number of sentences per cluster, these methods generate good results because clusters are composed of similar sentences with a high level of redundancy. LSI uses Singular-Value Decomposition (SVD), a technique closely related to eigenvector decomposition and factor analysis, to model the associative relationships (Deerwester et al., 1990). LDA is a topic model that generates topics based on word frequency from a set of documents (Blei et al., 2003). Finally, TextRank algorithm analyzes the words in texts using WGs and estimates their relevance (Mihalcea and Tarau, 2004). For LDA whose modeling is based on the concept of topics, we consider that the document D describes only one topic since it is composed of semantically close sentences. A same word or keyword can be represented by one or several nodes in WGs (see the WG construction in (Filippova, 2010)). In order to prioritize the sentence generation containing keywords, we add a bonus to the compression score when the compression contains different keywords. This process favors informativeness but may neglect grammaticality. Therefore, we also analyze 3-grams and compute in the graph their relevance scores.

The presence of a word in different sentences is assumed to increase its relevance for the MSC (we do not analyze stopwords). Thus, we define the relevance of a word i according to Equation 3.

$$1\text{-grams}(i) = \frac{\text{freq}(i)}{|D|_w} \times \frac{\text{freq}_s(i)}{|D|_s} \qquad (3)$$

where $\text{freq}_s(i)$ is the number of sentences containing the word i, $|D|_w$ and $|D|_s$ are the overall number of word occurrences and the number of sentences in the document D, respectively. Since we analyze Word Graphs whose basic connections are arcs associated with 2-grams, we define the relevance of 3-grams[2] from the inner 2-grams (Eq. 4 and 5).

$$\begin{aligned} 3\text{-grams}(i, j, k) = \text{freq}_3(i, j, k) \times \\ \frac{2\text{-grams}(i, j) + 2\text{-grams}(j, k)}{2} \end{aligned} \qquad (4)$$

---

[2]Since clusters are small, they have a limited number of sequences of an order higher than 3. Therefore, the use of 4-grams increases the complexity of the model without improving the quality of compression.

$$2\text{-grams}(i,j) = \frac{1\text{-grams}(i) + 1\text{-grams}(j)}{2} \quad (5)$$

where $\text{freq}_3(i,j,k)$ is the amount of 3-grams composed of the words i, j and k in the document. Taking into account frequent 3-grams aims at improving the grammatical quality of MSC while keeping the relevant information. The 3-grams bonus is obtained from the relevance of the 3-grams (Eq. 4).

3.2 Vertex-Labeled Graph

A vertex-labeled graph is a graph $G = (V, A)$ with a label on the vertices $K \to \{0, ..., nc\}$, where nc is the number of different labels. This graph type has been employed in several domains such as biology (Zheng et al., 2011) or NLP (Bruckner et al., 2013). In this last study, the correction of Wikipedia inter-language links was modeled as a Colorful Components problem. Given a vertex-colored graph, the Colorful Components problem aims at finding the minimum-size edge sets that are connected and do not have two vertices with the same color.

In the context of MSC, we want to generate a short informative compression where keyword may be represented by several nodes in the word graph. Labels enable us to represent keywords in vertex-labeled graphs and generate a compression without repeated keywords while preserving the informativeness. In this framework we grant bonuses only once for nodes with the same label to prioritize new information in the compression. To make our model coherent, we added a base label (label 0) for all non-keywords in the word graph. The following section describes our ILP model to select sentences inside WGs by taking into account 3-grams and labeled keywords.

3.3 ILP Modeling

We denote K as the set of labels, each representing a keyword, and A as the set of arcs in the WG. T is defined as the set of the 3-grams occurring more than once.

There are several algorithms with a polynomial complexity to find the shortest path in a graph. However, the restriction on the minimum number $P_{\min}$ of vertices (i.e. the minimum number of words in the compression) makes the problem NP-hard. Indeed, let v_0 be the "begin" vertex. If $P_{\min}$ equals $|V|$ and if we add an auxiliary arc from "end" vertex to v_0, our problem is similar to the Traveling Salesman Problem (TSP), which is NP-Hard.

For this work we use the formulation known as Miller-Tucker-Zemlin (MTZ) to solve our problem (Öncan et al., 2009; Thadani and McKeown, 2013). This formulation uses a set of auxiliary variables, one for each vertex in order to prevent a vertex from being visited more than once in the cycle and a set of arc restrictions.

The problem of production of a compression that favors informativeness and grammaticality is expressed as Equation 6. In other words, we look for a path (sentence) that has a good cohesion and contains a maximum of labels (keywords) and relevant 3-grams.

$$\min \left(\sum_{(i,j) \in A} w(i,j) \cdot x_{i,j} - c \cdot \sum_{k \in K} b_k - \sum_{t \in T} d_t \cdot z_t \right)$$
$$(6)$$

where x_{ij} indicates the existence of the arc (i,j) in the solution, $w(i,j)$ is the arc weight between the words i and j (Equation 1), z_t indicates the existence of the 3-grams t in the solution, d_t is the relevance of the 3-grams t (Equation 4), b_k indicates the existence of a word with label (keyword) k in the solution and c is the keyword bonus of the graph[3].

3.4 Structural Constraints

We describe the structural constraints for the problem of consistency in compressions and define the bounds of the variables. First, we consider the problem of consistency which requires an inner and an outer arc active for every word used in the solution, where y_v indicates the existence of the vertex v in the solution.

$$\sum_{i \in \delta^+(v)} x_{vi} = y_v \qquad \forall v \in V, \quad (7)$$

$$\sum_{i \in \delta^-(v)} x_{iv} = y_v \qquad \forall v \in V. \quad (8)$$

The second requirement for consistency associates 3-grams and 2-grams variables. We have a 3-gram (a, b, c) only if the 2-grams (a, b) and (b, c) are used.

---

[3]The keyword bonus allows the generation of longer compressions that are more informative.

$$2z_t \leq x_{ij} + x_{jl}, \qquad \forall t = (i, j, l) \in T. \tag{9}$$

The constraint (10) controls the minimum number of vertices ($P_{\min}$) used in the solution.

$$\sum_{v \in V} y_v \geq P_{\min}. \tag{10}$$

The set of constraints (11) matches label variables (keywords) with vertices (words), where $V(k)$ is the set of all vertices with label k.

$$\sum_{v \in V(k)} y_v \geq b_k, \qquad \forall k \in K. \tag{11}$$

Equality (12) sets the vertex v_0 in the solution.

$$y_0 = 1. \tag{12}$$

The restrictions (13) and (14) are responsible for the elimination of sub-cycles, where u_v ($\forall v \in V$) are auxiliary variables for the elimination of sub-cycles and M is a large number (e.g. $M = |V|$).

$$u_0 = 1, \tag{13}$$
$$u_i - u_j + 1 \leq M - M \cdot x_{ij} \quad \forall (i, j) \in A, j \neq 0. \tag{14}$$

Finally, equations (15) – (18) define the field of variables.

$$x_{ij} \in \{0, 1\}, \qquad \forall (i, j) \in A, \tag{15}$$
$$z_t \in \{0, 1\}, \qquad \forall t \in T, \tag{16}$$
$$y_v \in \{0, 1\}, \qquad \forall v \in V, \tag{17}$$
$$u_v \in \{1, 2, \ldots, |V|\}, \qquad \forall v \in V. \tag{18}$$

We calculate the 50 best solutions according to the objective (6) having at least 8 words and at least one verb. Specifically, we find the best solution, then we add a constraint in the model to avoid this solution and repeat this process 50 times to find the other solutions.

The optimized score (Equation 6) does not explicitly take into account the size of the generated sentence. Contrary to Filippova's method, sentences may have a negative score because we subtract from the cohesion value of the path the introduced scores for keywords and 3-grams. Therefore, we use the exponential function to ensure a score greater than zero. Finally, we select the sentence with the lowest final score (Equation 19) as the best compression.

$$\text{score}_{norm}(s) = \frac{e^{\text{score}_{opt}(s)}}{|s|}, \tag{19}$$

where $\text{score}_{opt}(s)$ is the score of the sentence s from Equation 6.

4 Experimental Setup

Algorithms were implemented using the Python programming language with the takahe[4] and gensim[5] libraries. The mathematical model was implemented in C++ with the Concert library and we used the solver CPLEX 12.6[6].

We define the keyword bonus as the geometric average[7] of all arc weights in the graph.

4.1 Evaluation Datasets

Various corpora have been developed for MSC and are composed of clusters of similar sentences from different source news in English, French, Spanish or Vietnamese languages. The corpora used by Filippova (2010) and Boudin and Morin (2013) contain clusters of at least 7 or 8 similar sentences, whereas the data of McKeown et al. (2010) and Luong et al. (2015) have clusters limited to pairs of sentences. McKeown et al. (2010) collected 300 English sentence pairs taken from newswire clusters using Amazon's Mechanical Turk. Like this previous study, Luong et al. (2015) used the same experimental setup to accumulate 115 Vietnamese clusters with 2 sentences by group. Boudin and Morin (2013), McKeown et al. (2010) and Luong

---

[4] http://www.florianboudin.org/publications.html

[5] https://radimrehurek.com/gensim/models/ldamodel.html

[6] CPLEX is available at: https://www-01.ibm.com/software/websphere/products/optimization/cplex-studio-community-edition/

[7] Each WG has different weight arcs, so it is important that keyword bonus has a correct value to allow the generation of slightly longer compressions. We tested several metrics (fixed values, arithmetic average, median, and geometric average of weights arcs of WG) to define the keyword bonus of WG and empirically found that the geometric average outperformed the others.

et al. (2015) made their corpora publicly available but only the corpus of Boudin and Morin (2013) is more suited to multi-document summarization or question-answering because the documents to analyze are usually composed of many similar sentences. Therefore, we use this corpus made of 618 French sentences spread over 40 clusters. Each cluster has 3 sentences compressed by native speakers, references having a compression rate of 60%.

4.2 Automatic and Manual Evaluations

The most important features of MSC are informativeness and grammaticality. Informativeness measures how informational is the generated text. As references are assumed to contain the key information, we calculated informativeness scores counting the n-grams in common between the compression and the reference compressions using the ROUGE system (Lin, 2004). In particular, we used the F-measure metrics ROUGE-1 and ROUGE-2, F-measure being preferred to recall for a fair comparison of various lengths of compressed sentences. Like in (Boudin and Morin, 2013), ROUGE metrics are calculated with stopwords removal and French stemming[8].

Due to limitations of ROUGE systems that only analyze 1-grams and 2-grams, we also led a manual evaluation with 5 French native speakers. The native speakers evaluated the compression in two aspects: informativeness and grammaticality. In the same way as (Filippova, 2010; Boudin and Morin, 2013), the native speakers evaluated the grammaticality in a 3-point scale: 2 points for a correct sentence; 1 point if the sentence has minor mistakes; 0 point if it is none of the above. Like grammaticality, informativeness is evaluated in the same range: 2 points if the compression contains the main information; 1 point if the compression misses some relevant information; 0 point if the compression is not related to the main topic.

5 Experimental Assessment

Compression rates are strongly correlated with human judgments of meaning and grammaticality (Napoles et al., 2011). On the one hand, too short compressions may compromise sentence structure, reducing the informativeness and grammaticality. On the other hand, longer compressions are more interesting for ATS when informa-

tiveness and grammaticality are decisive features. Consequently, we generate two kinds of compressions according to the number of keywords in the graph (5 or 10), which acts on the final size of the output sentences. The result tables are split into two parts, each having similar CRs and calculated from LSI, LDA or TextRank methods to identify the keywords of the clusters.

5.1 Results

Table 1 describes the results for the French corpus using ROUGE. The first two lines display the evaluation of the two baseline systems; the ROUGE scores measured with our method using either 5 or 10 keywords are shown in the next three lines and the last three lines respectively.

Globally, our ILP method outperforms both baselines according to ROUGE F-measures, but mostly using 10 keywords with higher CRs. The use of LDA and LSI to determine keywords gives better results than TextRank. ILP+LDA.5 and ILP+LSI.5 were better than the baselines for ROUGE-1 but the second baseline system generated shorter sentences with a better ROUGE-2 score.

We led a further manual evaluation to study the informativeness and grammaticality of compressions. We measured inter-rater agreement on the judgments we collected, obtaining the value of Fleiss' kappa of 0.303. This result shows that human evaluation is rather subjective. Questioning evaluators on how they proceed to rate sentences reveals that they often made their choice by comparing outputs for a given cluster.

Table 1 also shows the manual analysis that ratifies the good results of our system. Informativeness scores are consistently improved by the ILP method, whereas grammaticality results measured on the three systems are similar. Filippova's method obtained the highest value for grammatical quality. However, our system led to informativeness scores better than the two baselines using 5 and 10 keywords.

Finally, the reranking method proposed by Boudin and Morin, based on the analysis of *keyphrases* of candidate compressions with TextRank, improves informativeness, but not to the same degree as our ILP model. Despite this gain, the method is limited to candidate sentences generated by Filippova's and is dependent on the TextRank method.

---

[8]http://snowball.tartarus.org/

Methods	Automatic Evaluation		Informativeness				Grammaticality			
	ROUGE-1	ROUGE-2	0	1	2	Avg.	0	1	2	Avg.
Filippova	0.6383^7	0.4423^7	11%	55%	34%	1.23	1%	26%	73%	*1.72*
Boudin et al.	0.6595^7	*0.4616^7*	6%	56%	38%	1.32	1%	31%	68%	1.68
ILP+LDA.5	0.6591	0.4383	11%	46%	43%	1.33	4%	24%	72%	1.67
ILP+LSI.5	*0.6615*	0.4368	9%	49%	42%	*1.34*	3%	28%	69%	1.65
ILP+TR.5	0.6576	0.4382	9%	54%	37%	1.28	4%	27%	69%	1.64
ILP+LDA.10	**0.6871**	0.4712	7%	45%	48%	**1.40**	2%	34%	64%	1.62
ILP+LSI.10	0.6862	**0.4713**	8%	43%	49%	**1.40**	2%	33%	65%	1.63
ILP+TR.10	0.6495	0.4355	10%	51%	39%	1.28	6%	33%	61%	1.54

Table 1: ROUGE results and manual evaluations on the French corpus. The results in italics represent the best results with CR closed to the baselines. The best ROUGE results are in bold.

5.2 Discussion

The measures done with both the automatic metrics ROUGE and human evaluations bring to light that the method used to select keyword acts on the performance of our ILP method. We investigated this through the analysis of selected keywords occurring in one of the reference compressions (LDA_5: 91%, LDA_10: 84%, LSI_5: 90%, LSI_10: 84%, TextRank_5: 69%, TextRank_10: 56%). As expected, a higher percentage of keywords can be found in the references when the top 5 instead of 10 are considered. In keeping with the performance evaluations, a significantly higher rate of keywords existing in the references is observed when using LDA or LSI rather than TextRank. This shows the prominent role of keyword selection for our MSC method. Most keywords identified by LDA and LSI methods are the same (around 91%) while the intersection of keywords between LDA and TextRank methods is around 50% (a similar level is measured for the intersection from LSI and TextRank). This overlap of keywords justifies the similar results produced by our method using LDA and LSI methods.

Short compressed sentences are appropriate to summarize documents; however, they may remove key information and prejudice the informativeness of the compression. For instance, for the sentences that would be associated with a higher relevant score by the ATS system, producing longer sentences would be more appropriate. Generating longer sentences makes easier to keep informativeness but often increases difficulties to have a good grammatical quality while combining different parts of sentences. The experimental results we presented in Section 5.1 indicate that scores on

3-grams provide a good stability for our method to generate grammatically correct sentences, even for longer compressions.

The length of the size of the sentences output by our ILP method can evolve as needed in two ways. Firstly, our method can ensure to keep enough information, through the number of considered keywords. Increasing this number generates longer compressions because our method tries to add more keywords. Table 2 presents the average size of compressions according to the used MSC setting. Globally, the size is increased by 2 words when using the second baseline with respect to the first one. Our ILP system generates sentences of the same size as the second baseline when labeling 5 keywords in WG and compressions longer by 2 when labeling 10 keywords, which is still a moderate increase. Moreover, Table 2 displays the number of keywords that are kept in the final compression and shows that for TextRank, less competitive than LDA and LSI, several keywords are discarded by the ILP score that also takes into account cohesion and 3-grams scores.

Secondly, our ILP model can include an explicit constraint over the compression size ($MaxSize$):

$$\sum_{v \in V} y_v \leq MaxSize. \tag{20}$$

---

[8]Although we used the same system and data as Boudin and Morin (2013) for the French corpus, we were not able to exactly reproduce their results. The ROUGE scores given in their article are close to ours for their system: 0.6568 (ROUGE-1) and 0.4414 (ROUGE-2), but using Filippova's system we measured higher scores than them: 0.5744 (ROUGE-1) and 0.3921 (ROUGE-2). In spite of these discrepancies, both ROUGE scores and manual evaluations (Table 1) led to the same conclusions as them, showing that their method outperform Filippova's.

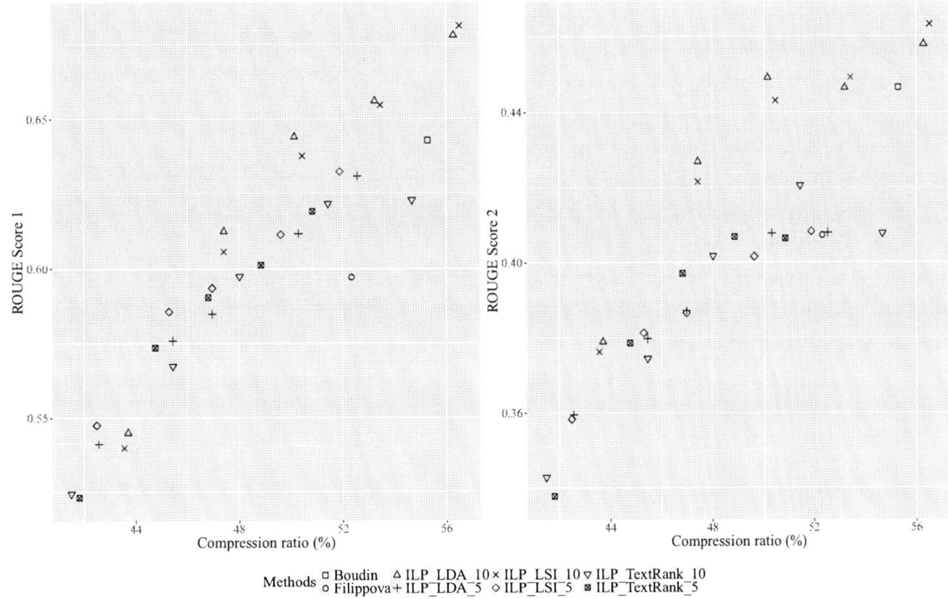

Figure 1: ROUGE recall for different maximum compression lengths using the French corpus.

| Methods | Length | | Keywords | CR |
	Avg.	Std.Dev.		
Filippova	16.9	5.1	—	52%
Boudin et al.	18.3	4.9	—	55%
ILP+LDA.5	18.7	7.0	4.6	56%
ILP+LSI.5	18.8	7.1	4.6	57%
ILP+TR.5	18.1	6.9	3.2	55%
ILP+LDA.10	20.7	6.7	8.2	62%
ILP+LSI.10	21.1	6.5	8.4	64%
ILP+TR.10	20.0	7.6	5.5	60%

Table 2: Compression length (#words), standard deviation and number of used keywords computed on the French corpus.

We set up our system to generate compressions with average lengths of 55%, 60%, 65%, 70% and 75% and report the results measured in terms of ROUGE with each setting in Figure 1. Unlike Table 1, we measure ROUGE recalls instead of ROUGE F-measures because these first metrics have a better correlation with informativeness and we already take into account the size of the produced sentences through CR.

First, let us note that the CRs effectively observed may differ from the fixed value of $MaxSize$. For example, a 55% threshold leads to real CRs of 42% to 44%, while a 65% level creates new sentences with a real CR between 47% and 51%. Interestingly, our system obtained better ROUGE recall scores than both baselines for comparable compression lengths. If we prioritize meaning, our method with 10 keywords improved the compression quality with a small increase of the compression length (compression ratio between 60% and 64%). Instead, we can limit the length of compressions and generate compressions that are shorter and have still better ROUGE scores than the baselines.

6 Conclusion

Multi-Sentence Compression aims to generate a short informative text summary from several sentences with related and redundant information. Previous works built word graphs weighted by cohesion scores from the input sentences, then selected the best path to select words of the output sentence. We introduced in this study a model for MSC with two novel features. Firstly, we extended the work done by Boudin and Morin (2013) that introduced keywords to post-process lists of N-best compressions. We proposed to represent keywords as labels directly on the vertices of word graphs to ensure the use of different keywords in the selected paths. Secondly, we presented a new relevance score for 3-grams to maintain grammaticality. We devised an ILP modeling to take into account these two new features with the cohesion scores, while selecting the best sentence. The compression ratio can be modulated

with this modeling, by selecting for example a
higher number of keywords for the sentences considered essential for a summary. Automatic measures with ROUGE package were supplemented
with a manual evaluation carried out by human
judges in terms of informativeness and grammaticality. We showed that keywords and relevant
3-grams are important features to produce valuable compressed sentences; in particular, testing
three different keyword selectors highlighted their
role in producing relevant sentences. The paths selected with theses features generate results consistently improved in terms of informativeness while
keeping up their grammaticality.

There are several potential avenues of work.
Following the system proposed by ShafieiBavani
et al. (2016), language models over POS can be
added as an additional score to the optimization
criterion to improve grammaticality. Another objective can be to manage polysemy through the use
of the same label for the synonyms of each keyword inside the Word Graph. Finally, MSC can be
jointly employed with classical methods of Automatic Text Summarization by extraction in order
to generate better summaries.

References

Siddhartha Banerjee, Prasenjit Mitra, and Kazunari
Sugiyama. 2015. Multi-document abstractive summarization using ILP based multi-sentence compression. In *IJCAI*. pages 1208–1214.

Regina Barzilay and Kathleen R. McKeown. 2005.
Sentence fusion for multidocument news summarization. *Computational Linguistics* 31(3):297–328.

David M. Blei, Andrew Y. Ng, and Michael I. Jordan.
2003. Latent Dirichlet allocation. *J. Mach. Learn.
Res.* 3:993–1022.

Florian Boudin and Emmanuel Morin. 2013.
Keyphrase extraction for N-best reranking in
multi-sentence compression. In *NAACL*. pages
298–305.

Sharon Bruckner, Falk Hüffner, Christian Komusiewicz, and Rolf Niedermeier. 2013. *Evaluation
of ILP-Based Approaches for Partitioning into
Colorful Components*, Springer Berlin Heidelberg,
Berlin, Heidelberg, pages 176–187.

James Clarke and Mirella Lapata. 2007. Modelling
compression with discourse constraints. In *EMNLP-
CoNLL*.

James Clarke and Mirella Lapata. 2008. Global inference for sentence compression: An integer linear
programming approach. *JAIR* 41:399–429.

Scott Deerwester, Susan T. Dumais, George W. Furnas, Thomas K. Landauer, and Richard Harshman.
1990. Indexing by latent semantic analysis. *Journal of the American society for Information Science*
41(6):391–407.

Katja Filippova. 2010. Multi-sentence compression:
Finding shortest paths in word graphs. In *COLING*.
pages 322–330.

Katja Filippova, Enrique Alfonseca, Carlos A. Colmenares, Lukasz Kaiser, and Oriol Vinyals. 2015.
Sentence compression by deletion with lstms. In
Lluís Màrquez, Chris Callison-Burch, Jian Su,
Daniele Pighin, and Yuval Marton, editors, *EMNLP*.
ACL, pages 360–368.

Katja Filippova and Michael Strube. 2008. Sentence fusion via dependency graph compression. In
EMNLP. pages 177–185.

Chin-Yew Lin. 2004. ROUGE: A Package for Automatic Evaluation of Summaries. In *Workshop Text
Summarization Branches Out (ACL'04)*. pages 74–
81.

A. V. Luong, N. T. Tran, V. G. Ung, and M. Q. Nghiem.
2015. Word graph-based multi-sentence compression: Re-ranking candidates using frequent words.
In *7th International Conference on Knowledge and
Systems Engineering (KSE)*. pages 55–60.

Kathleen McKeown, Sara Rosenthal, Kapil Thadani,
and Coleman Moore. 2010. Time-efficient creation
of an accurate sentence fusion corpus. In *HLT-
NAACL*. pages 317–320.

Yishu Miao and Phil Blunsom. 2016. Language as a
latent variable: Discrete generative models for sentence compression. In *EMNLP*. pages 319–328.

R. Mihalcea and P. Tarau. 2004. TextRank: Bringing
order into texts. In *EMNLP*.

Courtney Napoles, Benjamin Van Durme, and Chris
Callison-Burch. 2011. Evaluating sentence compression: Pitfalls and suggested remedies. In
*Workshop on Monolingual Text-To-Text Generation
(MTTG)*. pages 91–97.

Temel Öncan, İ Kuban Altınel, and Gilbert Laporte.
2009. A comparative analysis of several asymmetric
traveling salesman problem formulations. *Computers & Operations Research* 36(3):637–654.

Alexander M. Rush, Sumit Chopra, and Jason Weston.
2015. A neural attention model for abstractive sentence summarization. In *EMNLP*. pages 379–389.

Elaheh ShafieiBavani, Mohammad Ebrahimi, Raymond K. Wong, and Fang Chen. 2016. An efficient approach for multi-sentence compression. In
Robert J. Durrant and Kee-Eung Kim, editors, *8th
Asian Conference on Machine Learning*. PMLR,
Hamilton, NZ, volume 63 of *Machine Learning Research*, pages 414–429.

Kapil Thadani and Kathleen McKeown. 2013. Supervised sentence fusion with single-stage inference. In *IJCNLP*. pages 1410–1418.

Juan-Manuel Torres-Moreno. 2014. *Automatic Text Summarization*. John Wiley & Sons.

Emmanouil Tzouridis, Jamal Nasir, and Ulf Brefeld. 2014. Learning to summarise related sentences. In *COLING, Technical Papers*. pages 1636–1647.

Chunfang Zheng, Krister Swenson, Eric Lyons, and David Sankoff. 2011. OMG! orthologs in multiple genomes — competing graph-theoretical formulations. In *WABI*. pages 364–375.

Large-scale spectral clustering using diffusion coordinates on landmark-based bipartite graphs

Khiem Pham
Department of Computer Science
San José State University
San José, California, USA
khiem.pham@sjsu.edu

Guangliang Chen
Department of Mathematics & Statistics
San José State University
San José, California, USA
guangliang.chen@sjsu.edu

Abstract

Spectral clustering has received a lot of attention due to its ability to separate nonconvex, non-intersecting manifolds, but its high computational complexity has significantly limited its applicability. Motivated by the document-term co-clustering framework by Dhillon (2001), we propose a landmark-based scalable spectral clustering approach in which we first use the selected landmark set and the given data to form a bipartite graph and then run a diffusion process on it to obtain a family of diffusion coordinates for clustering. We show that our proposed algorithm can be implemented based on very efficient operations on the affinity matrix between the given data and selected landmarks, thus capable of handling large data. Finally, we demonstrate the excellent performance of our method by comparing with the state-of-the-art scalable algorithms on several benchmark data sets.

1 Introduction

Given a data set $X = \{x_1, \ldots, x_n\} \subset \mathbb{R}^d$ and a similarity function $\delta(\cdot, \cdot)$ such as the Gaussian radial basis function (RBF), spectral clustering (von Luxburg, 2007) first constructs a pairwise similarity matrix

$$W = (w_{ij}) \in \mathbb{R}^{n \times n}, \quad w_{ij} = \delta(x_i, x_j) \quad (1)$$

and then uses the top eigenvectors of W (after certain kind of normalization) to embed X into a low-dimensional space where k-means is employed to group the data into k clusters. Though mathematically quite simple, spectral clustering can easily adapt to nonconvex geometries and accurately separate various non-intersecting shapes. As a result, it has been successfully applied to many practical tasks, e.g., image segmentation (Shi and Malik, 2000) and document clustering (Dhillon, 2001), often significantly outperforming

traditional methods (such as k-means). Furthermore, spectral clustering has a very rich theory (von Luxburg, 2007), with interesting connections to kernel k-means (Dhillon et al., 2004), random walk (Meila and Shi, 2001), graph cut (Shi and Malik, 2000) (and the underlying spectral graph theory (Chung, 1996)), and matrix perturbation analysis (Ng et al., 2001).

However, spectral clustering is known to suffer from a high computational cost associated with the $n \times n$ matrix W, especially when n is large. Consequently, there has been considerable effort to develop fast, approximate algorithms that can handle large data sets (Fowlkes et al., 2004; Yan et al., 2009; Sakai and Imiya, 2009; Wang et al., 2009; Chen and Cai, 2011; Wang et al., 2011; Tasdemir, 2012; Choromanska et al., 2013; Cai and Chen, 2015; Moazzen and Tasdemir, 2016; Chen, 2018). Interestingly, a considerable fraction of them use a landmark set to help reduce the computational complexity of spectral clustering. Specifically, they first find a small set of data representatives (called *landmarks*), $Y = \{y_1, \ldots, y_m\} \subset \mathbb{R}^d$ (with $m \ll n$), from the given data in X and then form an affinity matrix between X and Y (see Fig. 1):

$$A = (a_{ij}) \in \mathbb{R}^{n \times m}, \quad a_{ij} = \delta(x_i, y_j). \quad (2)$$

Afterwards, different scalable methods use the matrix A in different ways to cluster the given data. For example, the column-sampling spectral clustering (cSPEC) algorithm (Wang et al., 2009) regards A as a column-reduced version of W and correspondingly use the left singular vectors of A to approximate the eigenvectors of W. However, they seem to consider only unnormalized spectral clustering, and it is unclear how they extend their technique to normalized spectral clustering (Shi and Malik, 2000; Ng et al., 2001). Another example is the landmark-based spectral

Proceedings of the Twelfth Workshop on Graph-Based Methods for Natural Language Processing (TextGraphs-12), pages 28–37
New Orleans, Louisiana, June 6, 2018. ©2018 Association for Computational Linguistics

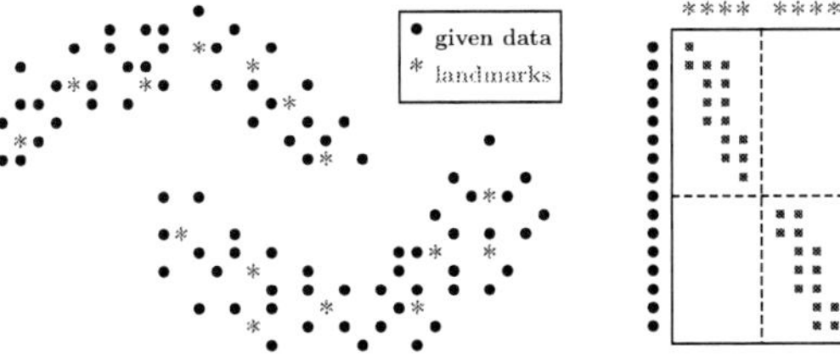

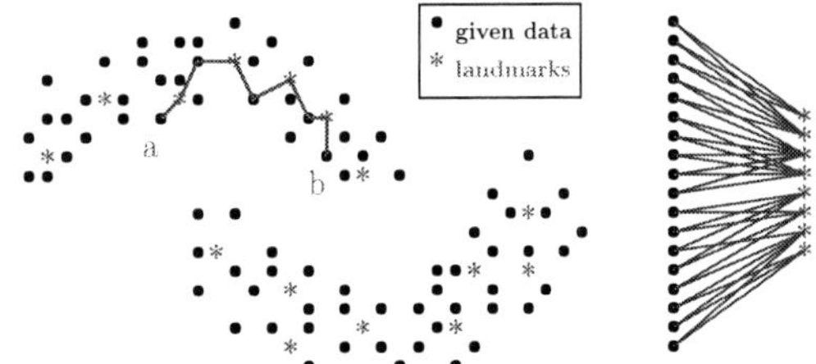

Figure 1: Illustration of landmark-based spectral clustering. Left: given data (in black color) and selected landmarks (in red); right: the affinity matrix A between the two sets of points with the blue squares indicating the largest entries in each row of A. Here, we assume that both the given data and the landmarks have been sorted according to the true clusters, so as to reveal the approximately block diagonal structure of A).

Figure 2: A bipartite graph whose two components are the given data (in black) and a landmark set learned from it (in red). Here, we form edges between each given data point and its two closest landmark points. Initially, no landmark point is connected to the two points a and b. However, if one simulates a random walk on the bipartite graph, then through a sequence of steps between the two components, a, b will be identified as belonging to the same cluster.

clustering (LSC) algorithm (Cai and Chen, 2015) which uses a row-sparsified version of the matrix A as approximate sparse representations of the input data while bypassing the expensive dictionary learning and sparse coding tasks. It then applies the L_1 normalization to each row of A, followed by a square-root L_1 column normalization. This method empirically works quite well but clearly there is a gap between its sparse coding motivation and the actual implementation. A third example is the k-means-based approximate spectral clustering (KASP) algorithm (Yan et al., 2009) which first applies the k-means algorithm to partition the given data into m small clusters and then performs spectral clustering to divide their centroids (which are the landmark points) into k groups. Next, they extend the clustering of the landmarks to the original data by performing 1 nearest neighbor (1NN) classification. This algorithm runs very fast, but is sensitive to the k-means clusters as it aggressively reduces the given data to a small set of centroids.

In this work we propose a novel landmark-based scalable spectral clustering approach by adapting the co-clustering framework by Dhillon (Dhillon, 2001) for landmark-based clustering and combining it with diffusion maps (Coifman and Lafon, 2006). Specifically, with the given data $X = \{x_i\}$ and a selected landmark set $Y = \{y_j\}$, we first construct a bipartite graph G_2 with X and Y being the two parts, and form edges between each x_i and its s nearest neighbors y_j in the landmark set with weights $a_{ij} = \delta(x_i, y_j)$. We then compute the transition probabilities for all the vertices of G_2 and use them to define a random walk on the bipartite graph, which (when being iterated for-

ward) further generates a diffusion process on G_2. We expect the resulting diffusion coordinates to be able to capture the global geometry of the clusters at different scales and, as a result, the connectivity of each cluster will be significantly strengthened (see Fig. 2). We will show that the diffusion coordinates may be computed directly from the $n \times m$ matrix $A = (a_{ij})$. Lastly, we propose three different ways to use the diffusion coordinates for clustering the data in X (depending on the length of the random walk).

The rest of the paper is organized as follows. First, in Section 2, we review some necessary background. We then present our methodology in Section 3. Experiments are conducted in Section 4 to test our proposed algorithms. Finally, we conclude the paper in Section 5.

2 Background

In this section, we first review the Normalized Cut (Ncut) algorithm (Shi and Malik, 2000) and its connections to random walk (Meila and Shi, 2001) and diffusion maps (Coifman and Lafon, 2006). Next, we will review the co-clustering framework in the setting of documents data by Dhillon (2001).

2.1 The Ncut algorithm

Given a data set $X = \{x_1, x_2, ..., x_n\} \subset \mathbb{R}^d$ and a notion of similarity δ, we may construct a weighted graph G by using the data points in X as vertices and assigning an edge between any two points x_i, x_j with associated weight $w_{ij} = \delta(x_i, x_j)$. Let $W = (w_{ij}) \in \mathbb{R}^{n \times n}$, which is the weight matrix of G. The degree of x_i is the total edge weight at that vertex: $d_i = \sum_j w_{ij}$, which measures the connectivity of x_i. The diagonal matrix $D = \text{diag}(d_1, \ldots, d_n)$ is called the degree matrix. The Laplacian of the graph G is defined as $L = D - W$, which is a positive semidefinite matrix. One way to normalize L is the following

$$L_{rw} = D^{-1}L = I - D^{-1}W. \tag{3}$$

For any subset of vertices $S \subset X$, we define the cut between S and its complement $\bar{S}$ as

$$\text{cut}(S, \bar{S}) = \sum_{x_i \in S} \sum_{x_j \in \bar{S}} w_{ij}. \tag{4}$$

The volume of S is defined as the total connectivity of the vertices in S:

$$\text{vol}(S) = \sum_{x_i \in S} d_i. \tag{5}$$

The Ncut algorithm (Shi and Malik, 2000) finds k clusters from the given data X by minimizing the following objective function:

$$\text{Ncut}(S_1, \ldots, S_k) = \sum_{\ell=1}^{k} \frac{cut(S_\ell, \bar{S}_\ell)}{vol(S_\ell)} \tag{6}$$

over all possible partitions $X = S_1 \cup \cdots \cup S_k$. Such a formulation of clustering is very convenient, however, the resulting optimization problem is intractable due to its combinatorial nature. Fortunately, by using a continuous relaxation, the above problem is reduced to finding the bottom $k - 1$ eigenvectors of the normalized graph Laplacian L_{rw} (corresponding to its smallest positive eigenvalues)[1]:

$$V = [v_1 \mid \cdots \mid v_{k-1}] \in \mathbb{R}^{n \times (k-1)}. \tag{7}$$

One then regards the rows of V as a low-dimensional embedding of the original data and clusters them by using k-means.

2.2 Random walk and diffusion maps

Let $P = D^{-1}W$, whose row sums are all one. We can then write $L_{rw} = I - P$. Algebraically, the bottom eigenvectors of L_{rw} are just the top eigenvectors of P. However, since P is row-stochastic, it can be used as a transition probability matrix to

---

[1]It can be easily shown that, for any weighted graph, the smallest eigenvalue of L_{rw} is $\lambda_0 = 0$, with associated eigenvector $v_0 = (1, \ldots, 1)^t$. This eigenpair is skipped by the Ncut algorithm.

define a random walk on the graph G (Meila and Shi, 2001). Under such a model, clustering can be interpreted as a way of finding a partition of the graph such that the random walk stays long inside the clusters and rarely moves between them.

If the random walk is moved forward for many iterations, then a diffusion process is generated on the graph G. For every integer $\alpha \geq 1$, P^α is the α-step transition matrix. Different values of α integrate the local connectivity information of the graph at different scales, with larger α yielding more global descriptions. The rows of P^α define a family of discrete distributions, one at each vertex of G, and are called the α-step diffusion coordinates (Coifman and Lafon, 2006). For practical purposes, it suffices to use low-dimensional approximations of them (by exploiting the fast decay of the α-th power of the spectrum of P):

$$V^{(\alpha)} = [\lambda_1^\alpha v_1 \mid \cdots \mid \lambda_p^\alpha v_p] \in \mathbb{R}^{n \times p}, \tag{8}$$

where $p \in \mathbb{Z}^+$ and λ_i, v_i are the largest eigenvalues and eigenvectors of P (excluding the eigenvalue 1 and associated eigenvector). In this work, we use the rows of $V^{(\alpha)}$ as an embedding of the data for clustering purposes.

2.3 Dhillon's co-clustering framework

Dhillon (2001) proposed a spectral clustering based co-clustering framework in the setting of documents clustering. Specifically, given a document-term frequency matrix $A \in \mathbb{R}^{n \times m}$, they first construct a bipartite graph G_2 whose two parts are the documents and terms, respectively, and then use A to define a weight matrix for G_2 as follows:

$$W = \begin{pmatrix} & A \\ A^t & \end{pmatrix} \in \mathbb{R}^{(n+m) \times (n+m)}. \tag{9}$$

The two empty blocks of W are zero matrices of appropriate sizes (which have been omitted for simplicity), indicating no connection among documents or terms. Afterwards, they apply the Ncut algorithm (along with the above weight matrix W) to co-cluster documents and terms, and they derived an efficient way to implement Ncut solely based on operations on the $n \times m$ matrix A (thus effectively avoiding the larger matrix W in all calculations). We review their derivation below.

We start with some definitions. First, let D_1, D_2 be two diagonal matrices consisting (resp.) of the row and column sums of A:

$$D_1 = \text{diag}(A\,1), \quad D_2 = \text{diag}(A^t\,1). \tag{10}$$

Here, and in what follows, we abuse notation to use 1 to denote the column vector (with appropriate dimension) with all entries equal to one. Next, we define three different normalized version of A:

$$\widetilde{A}_1 = D_1^{-1} A, \quad \widetilde{A}_2 = A D_2^{-1}, \qquad (11)$$

$$\widetilde{A} = D_1^{-1/2} A D_2^{-1/2}. \qquad (12)$$

It is easy to see that $\widetilde{A}_1, \widetilde{A}_2$ are respectively row- and column-stochastic, while $\widetilde{A}$ is closely related to both of them in the following ways:

$$\widetilde{A}_1 = D_1^{-1/2} \widetilde{A} D_2^{1/2}, \qquad (13)$$

$$\widetilde{A}_2 = D_1^{1/2} \widetilde{A} D_2^{-1/2}. \qquad (14)$$

The degree matrix of the bipartite graph is

$$D = \mathrm{diag}(W\, 1) = \begin{pmatrix} D_1 & \\ & D_2 \end{pmatrix}, \qquad (15)$$

from which we may obtain the following transition probability matrix for the bipartite graph:

$$P = D^{-1} W = \begin{pmatrix} & \widetilde{A}_1 \\ \widetilde{A}_2^t & \end{pmatrix}. \qquad (16)$$

The following result, first proved by Dhillon (2001), indicates the close connection between the eigenvalue decomposition of P and the SVD of $\widetilde{A}$.

Lemma 1. *Let $v_1 \in \mathbb{R}^n$, $v_2 \in \mathbb{R}^m$ and $v = (v_1; v_2) \in \mathbb{R}^{n+m}$. Then v is an eigenvector of P if and only if $\widetilde{v}_1 = D_1^{1/2} v_1$ and $\widetilde{v}_2 = D_2^{1/2} v_2$ are a pair of left/right singular vectors of $\widetilde{A}$.*

Proof. Suppose v is an eigenvector of P corresponding to some eigenvalue λ, that is, $Pv = \lambda v$, or equivalently,

$$\begin{bmatrix} & \widetilde{A}_1 \\ \widetilde{A}_2^t & \end{bmatrix} \begin{bmatrix} v_1 \\ v_2 \end{bmatrix} = \lambda \begin{bmatrix} v_1 \\ v_2 \end{bmatrix}, \qquad (17)$$

From this we obtain

$$\widetilde{A}_1 v_2 = \lambda v_1, \quad \widetilde{A}_2^t v_1 = \lambda v_2 \qquad (18)$$

and also (after plugging in (13) and (14))

$$\widetilde{A} D_2^{1/2} v_2 = \lambda D_1^{1/2} v_1, \qquad (19)$$

$$\widetilde{A}^t D_1^{1/2} v_1 = \lambda D_2^{1/2} v_2. \qquad (20)$$

This shows that $D_1^{1/2} v_1$ and $D_2^{1/2} v_2$ are the left and right singular vectors of $\widetilde{A}$ (corresponding to the same singular value λ). It is easy to verify that the converse is also true. $\qquad\square$

Therefore, to obtain an eigenvector of P, we just need to first perform the SVD of $\widetilde{A}$ to find a pair of its left and right singular vectors

$$\widetilde{v}_1 = D_1^{1/2} v_1, \quad \widetilde{v}_2 = D_2^{1/2} v_2, \qquad (21)$$

and then apply the following formula

$$v = \begin{pmatrix} v_1 \\ v_2 \end{pmatrix} = \begin{pmatrix} D_1^{-1/2} \widetilde{v}_1 \\ D_2^{-1/2} \widetilde{v}_2 \end{pmatrix} = D^{-1/2} \widetilde{v}, \qquad (22)$$

where $\widetilde{v} = (\widetilde{v}_1; \widetilde{v}_2) \in \mathbb{R}^{n+m}$.

Lastly, to complete the co-clustering task, one just stacks the top $k - 1$ eigenvectors of P as columns to form an embedding matrix $\mathbb{V} \in \mathbb{R}^{(n+m)\times(k-1)}$ and applies k-means to its rows to group the documents and terms simultaneously.

3 Methodology

In the previous section we reviewed the co-clustering framework by Dhillon (2001) which employs the Ncut algorithm (Shi and Malik, 2000) to partition a bipartite graph consisting of documents and terms by directly working on the document-term matrix. In this section, we extend their work in two ways. First, we adapt their bipartite graph model for landmark-based clustering by using instead the given data and a selected landmark set as its two parts. Second, we simulate a diffusion process on the bipartite graph to gather global information about the graph, however, our focus is still on clustering the given data for which we will introduce several ways of using such a bipartite graph model.

3.1 Derivation of diffusion coordinates on a bipartite graph

Given a data set, $X = \{x_1, \ldots, x_n\} \subset \mathbb{R}^d$, to be partitioned into k clusters, we select from X a set of landmark points, $Y = \{y_1, \ldots, y_m\} \subset \mathbb{R}^d$ (with $m \ll n$), by some sampling method, such as uniform sampling or k-means clustering. Let $A \in \mathbb{R}^{n\times m}$ be the affinity matrix between X and Y, computed by using a pre-specified similarity function δ as in (2). Like LSC (Cai and Chen, 2015), we preserve only the largest s ($s \ll m$) entries in each row of A, but our motivation is to focus on the most similar landmark points for each given data point. We then construct a bipartite graph $G_{X,Y}$ with X, Y as its two parts and a weight matrix W of the form in (9) but based on the affinity matrix A defined above. Again, the two empty blocks of W indicate no connection inside each component of $G_{X,Y}$. Also, the s-sparse rows of A imply that each point in X is only connected to its s nearest neighbors in Y on the bipartite graph. See Fig. 2 for an illustration of our bipartite graph model.

Using the computational framework laid out in Subsec. 2.3, we may easily obtain various quantities like $\widetilde{A}_1, \widetilde{A}_2, \widetilde{A}, D, P$. In particular, we may use the transition matrix P to define a random walk on the bipartite graph and run it forward continuously to generate a diffusion process. The α-step transition matrix, P^α has the following form.

Lemma 2. *Let $\alpha \geq 1$ be any integer.*
(1) If $\alpha = 2q$ is even, then

$$P^\alpha = \begin{pmatrix} \left(\widetilde{A}_1 \widetilde{A}_2^t\right)^q & \\ & \left(\widetilde{A}_2^t \widetilde{A}_1\right)^q \end{pmatrix} \qquad (23)$$

(2) If $\alpha = 2q + 1$ is odd, then

$$P^\alpha = \begin{pmatrix} & \left(\widetilde{A}_1 \widetilde{A}_2^t\right)^q \widetilde{A}_1 \\ \left(\widetilde{A}_2^t \widetilde{A}_1\right)^q \widetilde{A}_2^t & \end{pmatrix} \qquad (24)$$

This result indicates that after an even number of steps, the random walk (no matter in which component of the bipartite graph it is initiated) is always back to the original component, so that the original bipartite graph becomes two disconnected subgraphs, while after an odd number of steps, the random walk always ends in the other component, and hence the graph remains bipartite. See Fig. 3 for an illustration. Also, when $\alpha = 2q$, the α-step random walk on the bipartite graph $G_{X,Y}$ is equivalent to a q-step random walk within each component of $G_{X,Y}$ with the transition matrix $\widetilde{A}_1 \widetilde{A}_2^t$ or $\widetilde{A}_2^t \widetilde{A}_1$. This implies that for even integers α, one should focus on the two components X, Y of the bipartite graph separately and in principle may use the corresponding blocks of P^α as new transition matrices for clustering the two sets of data individually. In contrast, for odd integers α, one still needs to consider the two components X, Y together as a bipartite graph and simultaneously cluster the original data and the landmark set.

The actual algorithm we will propose uses a family of diffusion coordinates (corresponding to different time steps of the diffusion process) to embed the input data and/or the landmark points into low-dimensional spaces for clustering by k-means. The next result shows that one may obtain

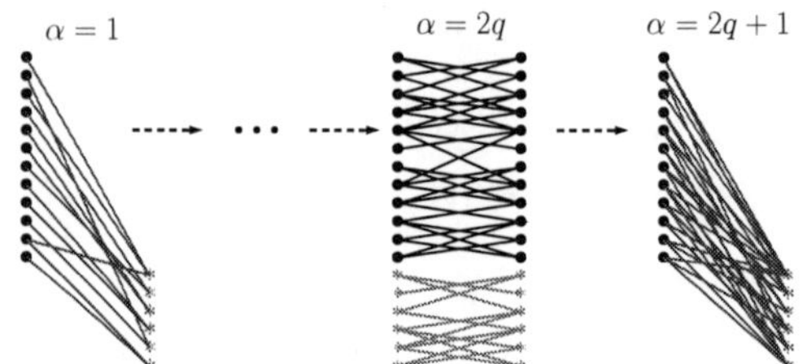

Figure 3: Simulation of a diffusion process on a bipartite graph. Left: initial bipartite graph; middle: the resulting graph after an even number of random walk iterations; right: the resulting graph after an odd number of iterations.

such diffusion coordinates directly from the matrix $\widetilde{A}$ (defined in (12)).

Theorem 1. *Let $\alpha, p \geq 1$ be two integers. The p-dimensional diffusion coordinates for $G_{X,Y}$ at time step α are*

$$\mathbb{V}^{(\alpha)} = D^{-1/2} \widetilde{V} \Lambda^\alpha \in \mathbb{R}^{(n+m)\times p}, \qquad (25)$$

where $\Lambda = diag(\lambda_1, \ldots, \lambda_p) \in \mathbb{R}^{p\times p}$ contains the largest p singular values of $\widetilde{A}$ (excluding the singular value 1), and $\widetilde{V} \in \mathbb{R}^{(n+m)\times p}$ the corresponding pairs of left and right singular vectors of $\widetilde{A}$ (one pair in each column).

Proof. This is a direct consequence of Lemma 1 combined with the formula in (8). $\square$

Remark. We fix $p = k - 1$ (where k is the number of clusters) in the rest of the paper (so as to be consistent with the Ncut algorithm (Shi and Malik, 2000)), but other values of p could be used too (e.g. those determined based on the actual power decay of the eigenvalues of P).

Remark. If we extend α to zero in (25), then we can obtain the embedding used by Dhillon (2001). This shows that our work extends (Dhillon, 2001).

Remark. When α is even, the top $n \times p$ and bottom $m \times p$ blocks of $\mathbb{V}^{(\alpha)}$, denoted as $\mathbb{V}_X^{(\alpha)}, \mathbb{V}_Y^{(\alpha)}$, may be used separately as diffusion coordinates for the two sets of data X, Y.

3.2 Proposed algorithm

We present several different ways to use the α-step diffusion coordinates $\mathbb{V}^{(\alpha)} \in \mathbb{R}^{(n+m)\times(k-1)}$ in (25), computed from a landmark-based bipartite graph $G_{X,Y}$, for clustering the input data X.

We consider the following two cases:
(1) α even: In this case, the initial bipartite graph becomes two disjoint subgraphs corresponding to

---

Algorithm 1 Landmark-based Bipartite Diffusion Maps (LBDM)

Input: Data set $X = \{x_1, x_2, ..., x_n\} \subset \mathbb{R}^d$, # clusters k, similarity function δ, landmark selection method, # landmarks m, # nearest landmarks s, # diffusion steps α, clustering method: direct or landmark (for even α), or co-clustering (for odd α).

Output: A partition of X into k clusters.

1: Find m landmarks $Y = \{y_1, \ldots, y_m\} \subset \mathbb{R}^d$ using the given method.
2: Form the affinity matrix A between the input data X and their respective s nearest landmark points in Y by using the given similarity function δ.
3: Calculate the row and column sums of A and use them to normalize A to obtain $\widetilde{A}$ (as in (12)).
4: Find the largest $k - 1$ singular values (excluding 1) and corresponding left and right singular vectors of $\widetilde{A}$.
5: Compute the diffusion coordinates matrix $\mathbb{V}^{(\alpha)}$ by (25) (with $p = k - 1$).
6: Use the indicated clustering method to divide the input data set X into k clusters.

X and Y, respectively. A direct way of clustering the input data X is to focus on $\mathbb{V}_X^{(\alpha)}$, the α-step diffusion coordinates for X, and apply k-means to group them into k clusters. Alternatively, we can focus on $\mathbb{V}_Y^{(\alpha)}$, the α-step diffusion coordinates for the landmark set Y, and use k-means to group the landmark points into k subsets. Afterwards, we extend the landmark clustering to the input data through s nearest neighbors (sNN) classification, where s is the number of closest landmark points connected to each data point.

(2) α odd: In this case, we are still left with a bipartite graph. To cluster the input data X, we propose to run k-means with the full set of diffusion coordinates $\mathbb{V}^{(\alpha)}$ to divide $X \cup Y$ into k clusters, and later remove the landmark points from them. We refer to the three above-mentioned methods for clustering the given data respectively as *direct clustering*, *landmark clustering*, and *co-clustering*.

We now present our scalable spectral clustering algorithm in Alg. 1.

Remark. We mention the work of Liu et al. (2013) in the setting of large graph data, which constructs a bipartite graph between the original graph nodes and "supernodes" generated through graph coarsening and then uses the plain co-clustering algorithm by Dhillon (2001) to partition the graph. Though the idea is somewhat similar, our method directly operates in the Euclidean data domain and extracts diffusion coordinates from the bipartite graph for clustering.

3.3 Run time analysis

The landmark selection step of Alg. 1 takes $O(ndm)$ time when k-means sampling is used, or $O(m)$ time when uniform sampling is used. The matrix A can be constructed in $O(nm(d + s))$ time since it takes $O(nmd)$ time to calculate all the pairwise distances between X and Y, and $O(nsm)$ time to find the s nearest landmarks in Y for each of the n data points in X. It then takes $O(ns)$ time to obtain $\widetilde{A}$, and $O(nsk)$ time to perform rank-k SVD of $\widetilde{A}$. The diffusion coordinates $\mathbb{V}^{(\alpha)}$ can be computed in $O((n + m)k)$ time. The final clustering step may take $O(nk^2)$, or $O(mk^2 + ns)$, or $O((n + m)k^2)$ time, depending on the clustering method. Putting everything together, the total running time is $O(nm(d + s) + nk(s + k))$.

4 Experiments

In this section, we conduct extensive experiments to evaluate the practical performance of LBDM with $\alpha = 1, 2$. For the odd value $\alpha = 1$, for which the co-clustering method has to be used, we denote the corresponding implementation by LBDM$^{(1)}$. For the even value $\alpha = 2$, we use both the direct clustering and landmark clustering methods and denote them as LBDM$^{(2,X)}$ and LBDM$^{(2,Y)}$, respectively.

4.1 Experimental setup

We compare the different LBDM versions with the following algorithms: KASP (Yan et al., 2009), LSC (Cai and Chen, 2015), cSPEC (Wang et al., 2009), and the co-clustering algorithm by Dhillon (2001) (used similarly as LBDM$^{(1)}$), in the setting of Gaussian similarity. We also include the plain Ncut algorithm (Shi and Malik, 2000) in our study (as a baseline). We implement all the methods in MATLAB 2016b (except LSC[2]) and conduct all

---

[2]MATLAB code available at http://www.cad.zju.edu.cn/home/dengcai/Data/Clustering.html

the experiments on a compute server with 48GB of RAM and 2 CPUs with 12 total cores.

We choose six benchmark data sets - *usps, pendigits, letter, protein, shuttle, mnist* - from the LIBSVM website[3] (see Table 1 for their summary statistics). They are originally partitioned into training and test parts for classification purposes, but for each data set we have merged the two parts together for our unsupervised setting. Also, we provide the true number of clusters k to all algorithms to focus on the clustering task.[4]

Table 1: Data sets used in our experiments.

Data	n	d	k
usps	9,298	256	10
pendigits	10,992	16	10
letter	20,000	16	26
protein	24,387	357	3
shuttle	58,000	9	7
mnist	70,000	784	10

In order to have a fair comparison between the different algorithms, we use the same values for the shared parameters. In particular, we fix $m = 500$ (for all methods) and $s = 5$ (for LSC, Dhillon and LBDM with $\alpha = 1, 2$). Also, we feed all the algorithms with the same landmark set found by k-means (with only 10 iterations), which is initialized with the centroids obtained by preliminary k-means clustering on 10% of the data (with 100 iterations, 10 restarts). In the last step of each algorithm (where k-means is applied to cluster data in the respective embedding space), we use 100 iterations and 10 restarts.

We evaluate the different methods in terms of clustering accuracy and CPU time (averaged over 50 replications), with the former being calculated by first finding the best match between the output cluster labels and the ground truth and then computing the fraction of correctly assigned labels.

4.2 Results

We report the experimental results in Tables 2 (accuracy) and 3 (time).

The following observations on the clustering accuracy are at hand: (1) LBDM$^{(2,Y)}$ achieved the

highest accuracy on three data sets (*usps, protein, mnist*), while LBDM$^{(2,X)}$ achieved the highest accuracy only on *letter*; (2) LSC and cSPEC each obtained the best accuracy once but each of them also performed very badly in at least one case; (3) The two co-clustering methods (Dhillon, LBDM with $\alpha = 1$) were very close and all performed reasonably well but never achieved the highest accuracy; (4) KASP never achieved the best accuracy either and performed very poorly in three cases (*pendigits, letter, mnist*). Overall, the LBDM family exhibited very stable performance (which demonstrates the power of diffusion coordinates), and they also outperformed the plain Ncut algorithm most of the time.

Regarding running time, LBDM$^{(2,Y)}$ and KASP are the two fastest methods because they both cluster the landmark points first and then extend the clustering to the input data through nearest neighbor classification. KASP is even faster because it applies spectral clustering directly to the landmark points in $\mathbb{R}^d$ (the corresponding weight matrix is only $m \times m$), but it is at the expense of accuracy. The cSPEC algorithm, on the other hand, is the slowest among the scalable methods (because it does not sparsify the matrix A), but it is still much faster than plain Ncut.

4.3 Parameter sensitivity study

We study in this section the effects of the parameters of LBDM (and relevant methods): m (number of landmark points), s (number of nearest landmark points), and α (diffusion time), using four data sets from Table 1: *usps, letter, protein,* and *mnist*.

In the first experiment, we focus on the parameter m by fixing $s = 5$ and varying m from 100 to 1000 with a step size of 100 in order to study its influence on all the scalable methods in Table 2. For each data set and each value of m, we apply k-means to sample m landmark points from the data set and provide the same landmark set to all the methods being compared to obtain their clustering accuracy and run time. This is then repeated 30 times and we report the average accuracy and time for each method in Fig. 4. In general, all methods except KASP and cSPEC improve their accuracy rates as more landmark points are used, with LBDM$^{(2,Y)}$ achieving the highest accuracy most of the time for three data sets (*usps, protein, mnist*). The CPU time of each algorithm seems to

<hr>

[3] https://www.csie.ntu.edu.tw/~cjlin/libsvmtools/datasets/

[4] When k is unknown, one may use methods like the gap statistic (Tibshirani et al., 2001) or eigenvectors rotation (Zelnik-Manor and Perona, 2004) to infer its value.

Table 2: Average clustering accuracy (%) of the various methods obtained on the data sets in Table 1. (Due to memory issue, we could not run the plain Ncut algorithm on the last two data sets.)

Dataset	Ncut	KASP	LSC	cSPEC	Dhillon	LBDM$^{(1)}$	LBDM$^{(2,X)}$	LBDM$^{(2,Y)}$
usps	66.21	67.25	66.86	66.89	68.21	67.80	68.10	_69.45_
pendigits	69.73	68.45	_77.93_	67.93	73.20	72.95	74.70	73.22
letter	24.93	26.19	31.51	24.98	32.06	32.13	_32.21_	31.28
protein	43.68	43.85	43.85	44.84	43.35	43.55	43.16	_45.88_
shuttle		74.52	39.71	_82.78_	74.24	74.26	74.38	74.49
mnist		57.99	70.28	54.50	72.15	72.43	72.37	_73.29_

Table 3: Average CPU time (in seconds) used by the various methods on the data sets in Table 1. The CPU time needed by the initial k-means to sample landmark points from each data set has been separately reported in the third column of the table (as it is common to all the methods).

Dataset	Ncut	(k-means)	KASP	LSC	cSPEC	Dhillon	LBDM$^{(1)}$	LBDM$^{(2,X)}$	LBDM$^{(2,Y)}$
usps	131.78	7.46 +	0.61	4.44	7.89	4.45	4.39	4.17	1.95
pendigits	246.08	3.13 +	0.55	3.08	5.26	3.14	2.91	3.08	1.65
letter	1180.70	5.30 +	0.77	12.24	25.07	13.51	14.96	12.87	2.78
protein	2024.54	27.04 +	0.41	3.55	7.54	3.93	4.04	3.93	4.40
shuttle		23.89 +	1.23	8.49	61.68	12.35	15.09	12.15	5.88
mnist		299.74 +	0.63	25.07	39.26	27.17	25.69	25.83	16.67

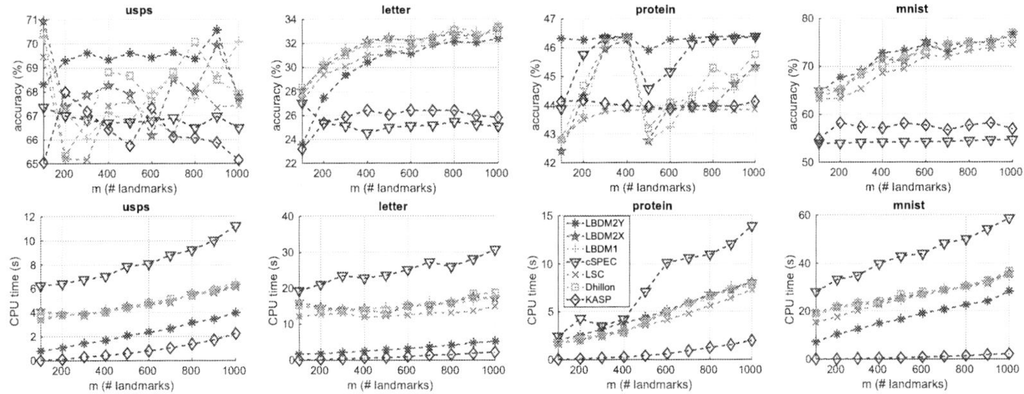

Figure 4: Effects of the parameter m (with $s = 5$ fixed all the time). Top row: clustering accuracy; bottom row: CPU time. In all plots the color and symbol of each method is fixed, so only one legend box is displayed.

depend linearly on m, with KASP always being the fastest two method.

In our second experiment about the parameter s (which is only needed by LBDM, LSC and Dhillon), we use the same setup as in the first experiment, except to fix $m = 500$ while varying s from 2 to 10 continuously. We plot the average clustering accuracy and run time of the different methods against the parameter s in Fig. 5. We see that increasing the value of s tends to decrease the clustering accuracy of each algorithm (with LBDM$^{(2,Y)}$ being the best in three cases), while increasing their run time linearly (but very little for LBDM$^{(2,Y)}$).

Lastly, we study the α parameter of LBDM by varying it from 1 to 40 continuously (with $m = 500$ and $s = 5$ fixed). Recall that for odd values of α, we have to use the co-clustering method LBDM$^{(\alpha)}$, while for each even value of α, we can use either the direct clustering method LBDM$^{(\alpha,X)}$ or the landmark clustering method LBDM$^{(\alpha,Y)}$. Their average accuracy (over 30 replications) for each value of α is displayed in Fig. 6. We can see that increasing the time scale α may further improve the clustering accuracy for all three methods on some data sets, demonstrating the power of diffusion maps.

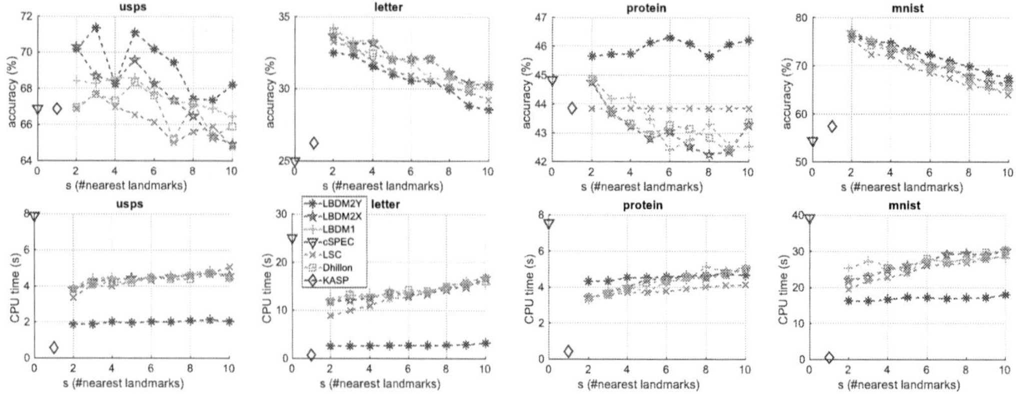

Figure 5: Effects of the parameter s (with $m = 500$ fixed all the time). Top row: clustering accuracy; bottom row: CPU time. Since KASP fixes $s = 1$ and cSPEC requires no sparsification, we have respectively plotted their accuracy rates at $s = 1$ and 0 in each plot.

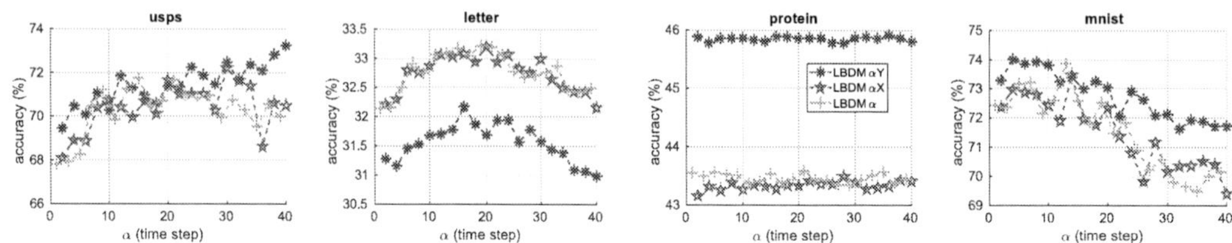

Figure 6: Effects of the parameter α on LBDM (with $m = 500$ and $s = 5$ fixed all the time).

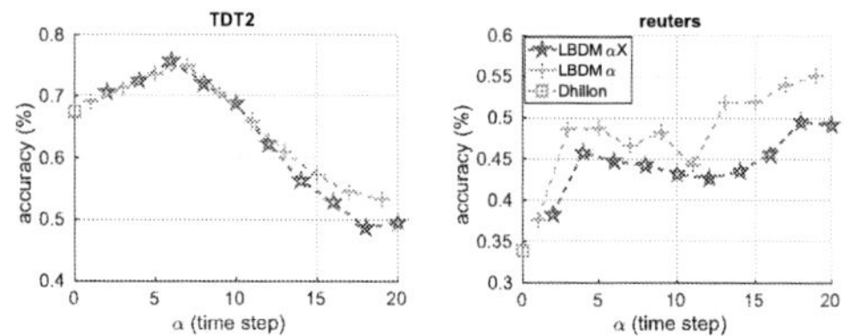

Figure 7: Clustering accuracy of LBDM (with $1 \leq \alpha \leq 20$) and Dhillon's method (shown at $\alpha = 0$) on two text data sets.

4.4 LBDM with bipartite graphs between documents and terms

In this section we conduct an extra experiment to show that we can easily adapt LBDM (Alg. 1) for the original bipartite graph model by Dhillon (2001), which consists of documents and terms, by simply treating the terms as the "landmarks" and using the document-term frequency matrix A as the affinity matrix between the two components of the bipartite graph. We then carry out the remaining steps of Alg. 1, using either the direct clustering method (for even α) or the co-clustering method (for odd α), and still denote them as LBDM$^{(\alpha,X)}$ and LBDM$^{(\alpha)}$.

We compare these two methods for $1 \leq \alpha \leq 20$ with Dhillon's co-clustering algorithm using two

news data sets, *TDT2* and *Reuters21578*.[5] Because of the much varied cluster sizes, we focus on the top 30 categories in each data set. The clustering accuracy of the three methods on both data sets is reported in Fig. 7. It is clear that the use of diffusion coordinates on the bipartite graph (for small α) considerably improves the documents clustering accuracy.

5 Conclusions

We presented a landmark-based scalable spectral clustering approach by a novel combination of diffusion maps and bipartite graphs. Our experiments showed that the proposed algorithm achieved very stable and competitive accuracy while running fast. We conclude that LBDM can be used as a very promising new alternative to current large-scale spectral clustering methods.

Acknowledgments

We thank the anonymous reviewers for helpful feedback. G. Chen was supported by a Simons Foundation Collaboration Grant for Mathematicians while conducting this research.

[5]Available at `http://www.cad.zju.edu.cn/home/dengcai/Data/TextData.html`

References

D. Cai and X. Chen. 2015. Large scale spectral clustering via landmark-based sparse representation. *IEEE Transactions on Cybernetics*, 45(8):1669–1680.

G. Chen. 2018. Scalable spectral clustering with cosine similarity. In *Proceedings of the 24th International Conference on Pattern Recognition (ICPR)*, Beijing, China. To appear.

X. Chen and D. Cai. 2011. Large scale spectral clustering with landmark-based representation. In *Proceedings of the Twenty-Fifth AAAI Conference on Artificial Intelligence*.

A. Choromanska, T. Jebara, H. Kim, M. Mohan, and C. Monteleoni. 2013. *Fast Spectral Clustering via the Nyström Method*, volume 8139 of *Algorithmic Learning Theory. ALT 2013. Lecture Notes in Computer Science*. Springer, Berlin, Heidelberg.

F. R. K. Chung. 1996. *Spectral graph theory*, volume 92 of *CBMS Regional Conference Series in Mathematics*. AMS.

R. Coifman and S. Lafon. 2006. Diffusion maps. *Applied and Computational Harmonic Analysis*, 21(1):5–30.

I. Dhillon. 2001. Co-clustering documents and words using bipartite spectral graph partitioning. In *Proceedings of the Seventh ACM SIGKDD International Conference on Knowledge Discovery and Data Mining*, KDD '01, pages 269–274, New York, NY, USA.

I. Dhillon, Y. Guan, and B. Kulis. 2004. Kernel k-means: Spectral clustering and normalized cuts. In *Proceedings of the Tenth ACM SIGKDD International Conference on Knowledge Discovery and Data Mining*, pages 551–556.

C. Fowlkes, S. Belongie, F. Chung, and J. Malik. 2004. Spectral grouping using the nystr'om method. *IEEE Trans. Pattern Analysis and Machine Intelligence*, 26(2):214–225.

J. Liu, C. Wang, M. Danilevsky, and J. Han. 2013. Large-scale spectral clustering on graphs. In *Proceedings of the Twenty-Third International Joint Conference on Artificial Intelligence*, pages 1486–1492. AAAI Press.

U. von Luxburg. 2007. A tutorial on spectral clustering. *Statistics and Computing*, 17(4):395–416.

M. Meila and J. Shi. 2001. A random walks view of spectral segmentation. In *Proceedings of the Eighth International Workshop on Artificial Intelligence and Statistics (AISTATS), Key West, Florida, USA*.

Y. Moazzen and K. Tasdemir. 2016. Sampling based approximate spectral clustering ensemble for partitioning data sets. In *Proceedings of the 23rd International Conference on Pattern Recognition (ICPR), Cancun, Mexico*. IEEE.

A. Ng, M. Jordan, and Y. Weiss. 2001. On spectral clustering: Analysis and an algorithm. In *Advances in Neural Information Processing Systems 14*, pages 849–856.

T. Sakai and A. Imiya. 2009. *Fast Spectral Clustering with Random Projection and Sampling*, volume 5632 of *Machine Learning and Data Mining in Pattern Recognition. MLDM 2009. Lecture Notes in Computer Science*. Springer, Berlin, Heidelberg.

J. Shi and J. Malik. 2000. Normalized cuts and image segmentation. *IEEE Trans. Pattern Anal. Mach. Intell.*, 22(8):888–905.

K. Tasdemir. 2012. Vector quantization based approximate spectral clustering of large datasets. *Pattern Recognition*, 45(8):3034–3044.

R. Tibshirani, G. Walther, and T. Hastie. 2001. Estimating the number of clusters in a data set via the gap statistic. *Journal of the Royal Statistical Society: Series B (Statistical Methodology)*, 63(2):411–423.

L. Wang, C. Leckie, R. Kotagiri, and J. Bezdek. 2011. Approximate pairwise clustering for large data sets via sampling plus extension. *Pattern Recognition*, 44:222–235.

L. Wang, C. Leckie, K. Ramamohanarao, and J. Bezdek. 2009. *Approximate Spectral Clustering*, volume 5476 of *Advances in Knowledge Discovery and Data Mining. PAKDD 2009, Lecture Notes in Computer Science*. Springer, Berlin, Heidelberg.

D. Yan, L. Huang, and M. Jordan. 2009. Fast approximate spectral clustering. In *Proceedings of the 15th ACM SIGKDD International Conference on Knowledge Discovery and Data Mining*, pages 907–916.

L. Zelnik-Manor and P. Perona. 2004. Self-tuning spectral clustering. In *Advances in Neural Information Processing Systems 17*, pages 1601–1608.

Efficient Graph-based Word Sense Induction
by Distributional Inclusion Vector Embeddings

Haw-Shiuan Chang[1], Amol Agrawal[1], Ananya Ganesh[1],
Anirudha Desai[1], Vinayak Mathur[1], Alfred Hough[2], Andrew McCallum[1]
[1]CICS, University of Massachusetts, 140 Governors Dr., Amherst, MA 01003
[2]Lexalytics, 320 Congress St, Boston, MA 02210

```
{hschang,amolagrawal,aganesh}@cs.umass.edu,
{anirudhadesa,vinayak,mccallum}@cs.umass.edu
al.hough@lexalytics.com
```


Abstract

Word sense induction (WSI), which addresses polysemy by unsupervised discovery of multiple word senses, resolves ambiguities for downstream NLP tasks and also makes word representations more interpretable. This paper proposes an accurate and efficient graph-based method for WSI that builds a global non-negative vector embedding basis (which are interpretable like topics) and clusters the basis indexes in the ego network of each polysemous word. By adopting *distributional inclusion vector embeddings* as our basis formation model, we avoid the expensive step of nearest neighbor search that plagues other graph-based methods without sacrificing the quality of sense clusters. Experiments on three datasets show that our proposed method produces similar or better sense clusters and embeddings compared with previous state-of-the-art methods while being significantly more efficient.

1 Introduction

Word sense induction (WSI) is a challenging task of natural language processing whose goal is to categorize and identify multiple senses of polysemous words from raw text without the help of predefined sense inventory like WordNet (Miller, 1995). The problem is sometimes also called unsupervised word sense disambiguation (Agirre et al., 2006; Pelevina et al., 2016).

An effective WSI has wide applications. For example, we can compare different induced senses in different documents to detect novel senses over time (Lau et al., 2012; Mitra et al., 2014) or analyze sense difference in multiple corpora (Mathew et al., 2017). WSI could also be used to group and diversify the documents retrieved from search engine (Navigli and Crisafulli, 2010; Di Marco and Navigli, 2013). After identifying senses, we can

train an embedding for each sense of a word. Li and Jurafsky (2015) demonstrate that this multi-prototype word embedding is useful in several downstream applications including part-of-speech (POS) tagging, relation extraction, and sentence relatedness tasks. Sumanth and Inkpen (2015) also show that word sense disambiguation could be successfully applied to sentiment analysis.

Since word sense induction (WSI) methods are unsupervised, the senses are typically derived from the results of different clustering techniques. Like most of the clustering problems, it is usually challenging to predetermine the number of clusters/senses each word should have. In fact, for many words, the "correct" number of senses is not unique. Setting the number of clusters differently can capture different resolutions of senses. For instance, race in the car context could share the same sense with the race in the game context because they all mean contest, but the race in the car context actually refers to the specific contest of speed. Therefore, they can also be separated into two different senses, depending on the level of granularity we would like to model.

For graph-based clustering methods, it is easy and natural to model the multiple resolutions of senses in a consistent way by hierarchical clustering and defer the difficult problem of choosing the number of clusters to the end. This makes it easier to incorporate other information, such as users' resolution preference on each hierarchical sense tree. The flexibility is one of the reasons why graph-based methods are widely studied and applied to many downstream applications (Mitra et al., 2014; Mathew et al., 2017; Navigli and Crisafulli, 2010; Di Marco and Navigli, 2013).

Nevertheless, graph-based WSI methods usually require a substantial amount of computational resources. For example, Pelevina et al. (2016) build the graph by finding the nearest neighbors

Proceedings of the Twelfth Workshop on Graph-Based Methods for Natural Language Processing (TextGraphs-12), pages 38–48
New Orleans, Louisiana, June 6, 2018. ©2018 Association for Computational Linguistics

of the target word in the word embedding space (i.e., ego network). Thus, constructing ego networks for all the words takes at least $O(|V|^2)$ time, where $|V|$ is the size of the vocabulary, unless some approximation is made (e.g., approximate nearest neighbor search such as k-d tree).[1] Next, if our goals include finding less common senses, the method needs to construct a large graph by including more nearest neighbors. For each target word, computing the pairwise distances between nodes in the large graph is also computationally intensive.

To overcome the limitations and make graph-based WSI more practical, we propose a novel WSI algorithm that first groups words into a set of basis indexes (i.e., a set of topics) efficiently and then, constructs the graph where each node corresponds to a basis index (i.e., a topic) instead of a word. The motivation behind the approach is that different senses of a word usually appear in different topics. For example, food and technology will be at least two distinct topics in most of the topic models, so we can find senses by clustering corresponding basis indexes safely when the target word is apple. If one word could have distinct senses in one topic, humans will constantly face difficult word sense disambiguation tasks while reading a document.

Although the main idea is simple, improving the efficiency significantly without sacrificing the quality is difficult. One of the challenges is that similarity between two basis indexes changes given different target words. For example, a country topic should be clustered together with a city topic if the target word is place. However, if the query word is bank, it makes more sense to group the country topic with the money topic into one sense so that the bank mention in Bank of America will belong to the sense. This means we want to focus on the geographical meaning of country when the target word is more about geography, while focus on the economic meaning of country when the target word is more about economics.

In order to tackle the issue, we adopt a recently proposed approach called distributional inclusion vector embedding (DIVE) (Chang et al., 2018). DIVE compresses the sparse bag-of-words while preserving the co-occurrence frequency order, so

DIVE is able to model not only the possibility of observing one target word in a topic as typical topic models but also the possibility of observing one topic of a sentence containing a target word mention. This allows us to efficiently identify the topics relevant to each target word, and only focus on an aspect of each of these topics composed of the words relevant to both the topic and the target word.

Experiments show that our method performs similarly compared with Pelevina et al. (2016), a state-of-the-art graph-based WSI method, without the need of expensive nearest neighbor search. Our method is even better for the words without a dominating sense.

2 Related Work

WSI methods can be roughly divided into two categories (Pelevina et al., 2016): clustering words similar to the target/query word or clustering mentions of the target word. We address their general limitations below.

2.1 Clustering Related Words

Graph-based clustering for WSI has a long history and many different variations (Lin et al., 1998; Pantel and Lin, 2002; Dorow and Widdows, 2003; Véronis, 2004; Agirre et al., 2006; Biemann, 2006; Navigli and Crisafulli, 2010; Hope and Keller, 2013; Di Marco and Navigli, 2013; Mitra et al., 2014; Pelevina et al., 2016). In general, the method is to first retrieve words similar or related to each target word as nodes, measure the similarity/relatedness between the words to form an ego graph/network, and either group the nodes by graph clustering or find hubs or representative nodes in the graph using HyperLex (Véronis, 2004) or PageRank (Agirre et al., 2006).

As we mentioned in the introduction section, building word similarity graph and performing graph clustering is usually computationally expensive unless relying on information other than co-occurrence statistics such as word snippets from a search engine (Navigli and Crisafulli, 2010; Di Marco and Navigli, 2013) or existing high-quality dependency parse (Mitra et al., 2014; Pelevina et al., 2016). Depending on the downstream applications and word similarity estimation algorithms available at the time of each work, the methods strive for the balance between efficiency and quality in different ways.

---

[1] Pelevina et al. (2016) also suggest that JoBimText is an efficient alternative to estimating word similarity, but the method still needs time to run a dependent parser and not every domain has an efficient and high-quality parser.

Most of the WSI methods that cluster words use graph-based algorithms. One notable exception is Lau et al. (2012). For each target word, they build a topic model, latent Dirichlet allocation or its extension, on the contexts of all mentions of target words. Although computing pairwise similarity is not required here, the approach is still computationally expensive because there might be tens of thousands of mentions of a target word in the corpus and the approach needs to train V different topic models instead of globally modeling topics once like our method.

In addition to the scalability concerns, we do not know how many mentions of a target word are semantically closest to each of its most related words (i.e., node in its ego-network). The loss of connection makes balance the cluster size during the clustering difficult. Furthermore, it might be common that when users would like to adopt fine-grained senses in the hierarchical clustering tree but realize that there is no mention in the corpus that would be categorized into some sense clusters.

2.2 Clustering Mentions

In addition to clustering words similar/related to the target word, we can also cluster every mention based on its context words, which co-occur in a small window. Although this way saves the time of finding similar words, the samples need to be clustered drastically increase because each target word could have tens of thousands of mentions in the corpus of interest. This makes bottom-up hierarchical clustering or global optimization such as spectral clustering (Stella and Shi, 2003) become infeasible. Without hierarchical sense clustering, it is hard to inject other sources of information such as user intervention or prior knowledge to determine the number of clusters.

To efficiently cluster many samples, Schütze (1992) sub-samples the context of mentions; Mu et al. (2017) run principle component analysis (PCA) to compress the contexts of each target word before clustering; other approaches adopt iteratively local search algorithms after random initialization such as expectation maximization (EM) (Reisinger and Mooney, 2010; Neelakantan et al., 2014; Tian et al., 2014; Piña and Johansson, 2015; Li and Jurafsky, 2015; Bartunov et al., 2016) or gradient descent (Athiwaratkun and Wilson, 2017). Although the random initialization and local search methods could be very ef-

ficient, the methods might suffer from bad local minimums. Moreover, the users need to specify the number of senses or a global hyper-parameter which controls the level of granularity at the beginning and hope that it will output the sense models with desired resolution after training finishes. The lack of a way to browsing different sense resolution limits the application of the type of WSI methods.

3 Method

The flowchart of our method is illustrated in Figure 1. We will first briefly introduce distributional inclusion vector embedding (DIVE) (Chang et al., 2018) in Section 3.1, illustrate how we use DIVE as a topic model to construct a graph in Section 3.2, and after clustering the topics, we explain the way to converting each topic cluster to a sense embedding in Section 3.3.

3.1 Distributional Inclusion Vector Embedding (DIVE)

Distributional inclusion vector embedding (DIVE) is a variation of skip-gram model (Mikolov et al., 2013). The two major differences compared with skip-gram are that (1) all word embeddings and context embeddings are constrained to be non-negative, and (2) the weights of negative sampling for each word is inversely proportional to its frequency. Specifically, the objective function of DIVE is defined by

$$l_{DIVE} = \sum_w \sum_c \#(w,c) \log \sigma(\mathbf{w}^T \mathbf{c}) +$$
$$k_I \sum_w \frac{Z}{\#(w)} \sum_c \#(w,c) \mathop{\mathbb{E}}_{c_N \sim P_D} [\log \sigma(-\mathbf{w}^T \mathbf{c_N})], \tag{1}$$

where the word embedding $\mathbf{w} \geq 0$, the context embedding $\mathbf{c} \geq 0, \mathbf{c_N} \geq 0$, $\#(w,c)$ are number of times context word c co-occur with w, $\#(w) = \sum_c \#(w,c)$, σ is the logistic sigmoid function, k_I is a constant hyper-parameter, Z is the average $\#(w)$ of all words (i.e., $Z = \frac{\sum_w \#(w)}{|V|}$ and $|V|$ is the size of vocabulary), and P_D is the distribution of negative samples. The two modifications do not change the time and space complexity of training skip-gram, which is one of the most scalable word embedding methods (Levy et al., 2015).

DIVE is originally designed to perform unsupervised hypernymy detection task, and its goal is to preserve the inclusion relation between two context features in the sparse bag of words

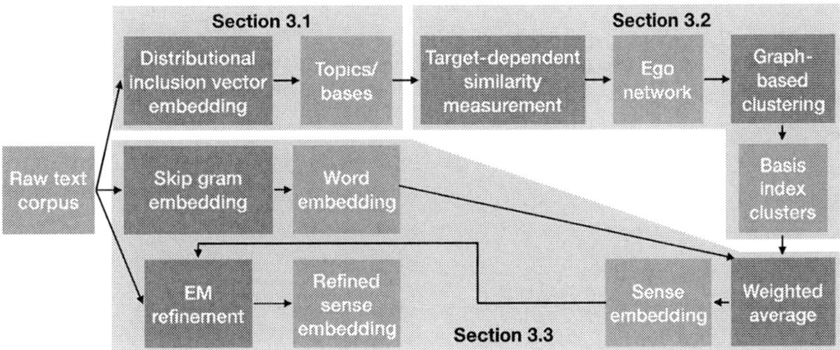

Figure 1: The flowchart of the proposed method. The blue boxes are processing steps, the orange boxes are input and output data of each step, and the gray areas indicate the sections describing the included steps.

(SBOW) representation. When the co-occurred context histogram of the word y includes that of the word x, it means that for all context words c in the vocabulary V, c will co-occur more times with y than with x. In this paper, the context words of a target word means the words co-occur with a target word mention within a small window in the corpus. The default context window size for DIVE is 10. Chang et al. (2018) show that the DIVE is able to compress the sparse bag of words while approximately preserving the inclusion in the low-dimensional space. Formally,

$$\forall c \in V, \ \#(x,c) \leq \#(y,c)$$
$$\overset{\sim}{\Longleftrightarrow} \forall i \in \{1, ..., L\}, \ \mathbf{x}[i] \leq \mathbf{y}[i], \quad (2)$$

where $\overset{\sim}{\Longleftrightarrow}$ means approximately equivalent, $\#(x,c)$ and $\#(y,c)$ are number of times context word c co-occurs with x and y, respectively. $\mathbf{x}$ and $\mathbf{y}$ are the embeddings of the words x and y, respectively, $\mathbf{x}[i]$ is the embedding value of in ith dimension (i.e., ith basis index). and L is number of DIVE basis indexes. See Chang et al. (2018) for more the derivation of the equation.

In order to satisfy equation (2), each basis index of DIVE corresponds to a topic and the embedding value at that index represents how often the word appears in the topic. This is because if the embedding of one word y has higher value in every dimension (i.e., higher frequency in every topic) than the value of another word x, the context words c in the topics usually co-occur more frequently with y than with x. Inversely, if x appears more often in one topic than y (i.e., the embedding value of x in the corresponding dimension is higher than that of y), some context words c in the topic could co-occur more often with x than

with y.

In Figure 2 (a), we present three mentions of the word **core** and its top 15 basis indexes in DIVE. The word that has a higher value in a basis index is more frequent in the corresponding topic. For example, the top 1-5 words in the second column of the table look more frequent (and usually more general) than the top 101-105 words.

3.2 Graph-Based Clustering

For each target word, we build an ego network whose nodes are the basis indexes relevant to the word. The basis index b is relevant if DIVE of the target word q has a value $\mathbf{w}_q[b]$ higher than a threshold T. The threshold is set to be 1% of average non-zero $\mathbf{w}_q[b]$ over basis indexes in our experiment.

Every pair of nodes are linked by an edge weighted by the similarity between the two basis indexes. Each basis index b_i is represented by a feature vector. A naive way to prepare the feature vector of ith basis index $\mathbf{f}_{(b_i)}$ is to use the embedding values in that index $\mathbf{w}[b_i]$ of all the words in our vocabulary V. That is,

$$\mathbf{f}_{(b_i)} = \underset{\mathbf{w} \in V}{\oplus} \mathbf{w}[b_i], \quad (3)$$

the operator $\oplus$ means concatenation. However, as discussed in Section 1, measuring similarity using the global features might group topics together based on the co-occurrence of words which are unrelated to the query words. Instead, we want to make the similarity dependent on the query word.

To create target-dependent similarity measurement, we only consider the embedding of words which are related to the query word as the features of basis indexes. Specifically, given a query word

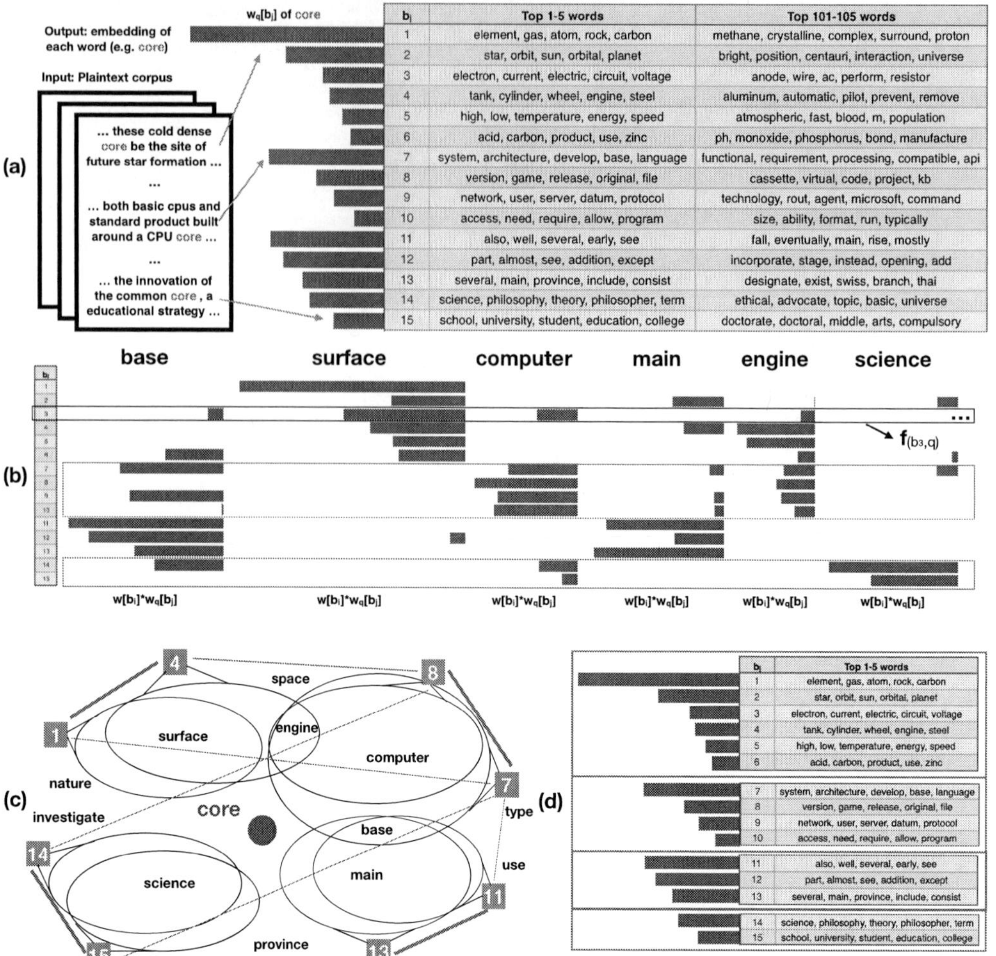

Figure 2: A visualization of finding the senses of the word **core**.
(a) The DIVE $\mathbf{w}[b_j]$ of the word **core** (only top 15 basis indexes are shown). The words in each row of the table are sorted by its embedding value in the basis index.
(b) Weighted DIVE of six words on these 15 basis indexes relevant to **core** as the features for measuring the similarity between basis indexes. The two red boxes indicate two final clusters we discovered at the end within which the feature words tend to have similar embedding values.
(c) The ego network constructed for the word **core**. Each blue box and the corresponding circle represent a basis index or topic (only 8 out of 15 basis indexes are plotted and their index numbers b_j are shown in the blue boxes), which is a node in the network. Two basis indexes are more similar if more relevant words (i.e., close to **core**) occur frequently in both corresponding topics. For example, the topic 7 and 8 are more similar because of the frequent appearance of the relevant words such as **computer** in both topics. The larger similarity is represented by a thicker red line. The ego network is a complete graph but only a subset of edges are plotted in the figure.
(d) The final clustering results when the number of clusters is set to be 4.

q, we only take the top n words of every basis index j in the set $B_j(n)$ instead of considering all the words in the vocabulary. Then, we weigh the feature based on how likely it is to observe the target word in topic j ($\mathbf{w}_q[b_j]$) and concatenate all features together. That is, the feature vector of the ith dimension $\mathbf{f}_{(b_i,q)}$ is defined as:

$$\mathbf{f}_{(b_i,q)} = \bigoplus_{j=1}^{L} \bigoplus_{\mathbf{w}\in B_j(n)} \mathbf{w}[b_i] \cdot \mathbf{w}_q[b_j], \qquad (4)$$

where n is fixed as 100 in the experiment.

In addition to decreasing the weight of irrelevant words, we also lower the influence of irrelevant bases by defining the similarity between two basis indexes as

$$SIM(b_i, b_j, q) = \cos(\mathbf{f}_{(b_i, q)}, \mathbf{f}_{(b_j, q)}) \cdot$$
$$\log(\frac{\min(\mathbf{w}_q[b_i], \mathbf{w}_q[b_j])}{T}), \quad (5)$$

where $\cos(\mathbf{f}_{(b_i, q)}, \mathbf{f}_{(b_j, q)})$ is the cosine similarity between the features of two basis indexes, and the term $\log(\frac{\min(\mathbf{w}_q[b_i], \mathbf{w}_q[b_j])}{T})$ is to prevent irrelevant basis indexes in the ego network misleading the clustering algorithm. Notice that $SIM(b_i, b_j, q) \geq 0$ because all features $\mathbf{f}_{(b, q)} \geq 0$ and every node is a relevant basis index b with $\mathbf{w}_q[b] > T$.

After the ego network is constructed, we could apply any hierarchical graph clustering. In this paper, we just choose spectral clustering with fixed number of clusters for simplicity. In our experiment, DIVE with 100 dimensions produces only 6.4 relevant basis indexes on average which needs to be clustered for each target word. This number goes to only 19 for DIVE with 300 dimensions. Thus, we are allowed to use spectral clustering to perform global optimization without inducing large computational overhead in this step.

In Figure 2, we use the target word core as an example to illustrate our clustering algorithm. After DIVE is trained in (a), we visualize six dimensions of features for each basis index $\mathbf{f}_{(b_i, q)}$ in (b). Using the features, we can build the ego network as shown in (c). The figure highlights the novelty of our approach. Instead of directly clustering words as other graph-based methods, we group the words first and cluster the groups to form senses. Since the basis is global, we do not have to retrain it given a different target word. DIVE provides us an easy and efficient way to ignore the irrelevant words being far away from core in (c), such as province or space, and cluster based on the words close to the target word such as main or computer. The target-dependent similarity measurement preserves the main spirit of existing graph-based approaches.

3.3 From Basis Index Clusters to Sense Embeddings

As shown in Figure 2 (d), every sense is represented by a group of basis indexes each of which has a weight based on its relevancy to the target word (e.g., the relevancy of b_ith basis index is $\mathbf{w}_q[b_i]$). In order to apply existing WSI evaluation

and potentially other downstream applications, we convert the basis index clusters to sense embedding.

First, we train a word embedding. Any existing embeddings could be used and we choose skip-gram due to its efficiency. Based on the trained word2vec, we first create a topic embedding for each basis index by averaging skip-gram embedding of the top 1000 words $B_i(1000)$ weighted by the DIVE $\mathbf{w}[b_i]$ of the words at b_ith basis index as given as:

$$\mathbf{t}_{b_i} = \frac{\sum_{\mathbf{w} \in B_i(1000)} \exp(\mathbf{w}'[b_i]) \cdot \mathbf{e}_w}{\sum_{\mathbf{w} \in B_i(1000)} \exp(\mathbf{w}'[b_i])}, \quad (6)$$

where $\mathbf{e}_w$ is the skip-gram embedding for the word whose DIVE are $\mathbf{w}$, and $\mathbf{w}'$ is normalized DIVE such that its average $\frac{\sum_{\mathbf{w} \in B_i(1000)} \mathbf{w}'[b_i]}{1000} = 1$. We take exponential on $\mathbf{w}'[b_i]$ to focus on the words that are more important to the b_i basis index because DIVE roughly models the log of word frequency in each topic (Chang et al., 2018).

To generate kth sense embedding $\mathbf{s}_k^q$ for a target word q, we take the average of all the topic embeddings in the kth sense cluster (found in Section 3.2) weighted by the relevancy between every topic and the target word. Specifically,

$$\mathbf{s}_k^q = \frac{\sum_{b_i \in S_k^q} \exp(\mathbf{w}'_q[b_i]) \cdot \mathbf{t}_{b_i}}{\sum_{b_i \in S_k^q} \exp(\mathbf{w}'_q[b_i])}, \quad (7)$$

where S_k^q is the set of basis indexes that belongs to the kth cluster, $\mathbf{w}'_q$ is normalized DIVE of the target word such that its average $\frac{\sum_{b_i \in N} \mathbf{w}'_q[b_i]}{|N|} = 1$, and N is the set of nodes in the ego network.

When converting clusters into embeddings, the previous graph-based WSI methods, such as Pelevina et al. (2016), average the embedding of related words. The average is effective in terms of discriminating the contexts of target word mentions, but it might not be a good embedding for the sense of target word itself. For instance, one sense embedding of core could be close to the embedding of computer, but the computer embedding does not represent the sense of core in computer context as well as the embedding of cpu. Our method suffers the similar problem.

To solve the issue, we use the sense embeddings from clusters as the initialization of an expectation maximization (EM) refinement. At E-step, we predict the sense of every target token by checking which sense embedding the average word embedding of the current sentence is closest to, and assign the sense to the target token (e.g., bank → bank_1). At M-step, we retrain the skip-gram using the updated corpus. Our refinement process could be seen as a simplified version of multi-sense skip-gram (MSSG) (Neelakantan et al., 2014), which can be easily implemented using existing word embedding library.

4   Experiments

We first conduct a qualitative experiment to verify that our clustering algorithm performs well on some typical polysemy, and show the results in Table 1. As we can see, our method can not only separate two senses in very different contexts but also can distinguish more subtle sense difference such as identifying the car context and competition context as two different senses of the target word race.

Intuitively speaking, our method could be especially useful when it comes to increase the recall of less common senses (like discovering the educational meaning of core), but it is hard to verify the claim using existing WSI benchmarks because the common senses, especially the most frequent sense, often dominate in the benchmarks unless using the datasets where the bias is removed. In the following sections, we will first introduce the setup and then the experiments on 3 datasets.

4.1   Experimental Setup

We train DIVE on first 51.2 million tokens of WaCkypedia (Baroni et al., 2009), the dataset suggested by Chang et al. (2018), and the default hyper-parameter setting is used except the number of embedding dimensions L (i.e., number of basis indexes). We train two DIVEs, one with 100 dimensions and the other with 300 dimensions to study how the granularity of basis affects the performance. For all other steps or baselines, we train them on the whole WaCkypedia where the stop words are removed.

For our clustering module, we use all the default hyper-parameters of the spectral clustering library in Scikit-learn 0.18.2 (Pedregosa et al., 2011) except the number of clusters is fixed at 2. Setting a number larger than 2 makes it harder to compare with the results generated from other baselines whose default hyper-parameters usually make average number of senses between 1 and 2. During EM, we train the skip-gram embedding on the

whole WaCkypedia where we treat every consecutive 20 tokens as a sentence, and the refinement stops after 3 EM iteration. In the tables of this section, our methods using DIVE with 100 and 300 dimensions are denoted as DIVE (100) and DIVE (300), respectively.

In all quantitative experiments, we compare our method with Pelevina et al. (2016), a state-of-the-art graph-based clustering which builds ego graphs based on words similar to the target words, so we call it word graph (WG). To train the model, we first train skip-gram on whole WaCkypedia and use all the default hyper-parameters in their released code to get sense embeddings.[2] We also apply our EM refinement step to their output embedding to make the comparison fair and call this variation WG+EM. We also compare our method with the baseline which randomly assigns two senses to every token and performs EM to refine the embedding (i.e., only adopting our post-processing step). The method is similar to multiple-sense skip-gram (Neelakantan et al., 2014), so we call it MSSG in our tables.

In all datasets, evaluation involves the similarity measurement between a sense of the target word and a context. For each query, we compute cosine similarity between the context embedding and the sense embedding of the target word, where the context embedding e_c is the average embedding of word in the context. Notice that each word in the context could also be polysemous. In these cases, we adopt the sense embedding of the context word that is closest to the sense of the target word (i.e., highest cosine similarity).

4.2   Word Context Relevance (WCR)

Given a target word, the task (Arora et al., 2016; Sun et al., 2017) is to identify the true context corresponding to a sense of the target word out of 10 other randomly selected false contexts, where a context is presented by similar words. For example, two of the true contexts for the target word bank are water,land,river,... and institution,deposits,money.... We use the R1 dataset from Sun et al. (2017), which consists of 137 word types and 535 queries.

For each query pair (target word w_q, context c), we compute the similarity between each sense of target word s_k^q and the context e_c, and choose the

---

[2]https://github.com/tudarmstadt-lt/sensegram

Query	CID	Top 5 words in the top dimensions	
rock	1	element, gas, atom, rock, carbon find, specie, species, animal, bird	sea, lake, river, area, water point, side, line, front, circle
	2	band, song, album, music, rock early, work, century, late, begin	write, john, guitar, band, author include, several, show, television, film
bank	1	county, area, city, town, west building, build, house, palace, site	several, main, province, include, consist sea, lake, river, area, water
	2	money, tax, price, pay, income united, states, country, world, europe	company, corporation, system, agency, service state, palestinian, israel, right, palestine
apple	1	food, fruit, vegetable, meat, potato war, german, ii, germany, world	goddess, zeus, god, hero, sauron write, john, guitar, band, author
	2	version, game, release, original, file system, architecture, develop, base, language	car, company, sell, manufacturer, model include, several, show, television, film
star	1	film, role, production, play, stage wear, blue, color, instrument, red	character, series, game, novel, fantasy write, john, guitar, band, author
	2	element, gas, atom, rock, carbon give, term, vector, mass, momentum	star, orbit, sun, orbital, planet light, image, lens, telescope, camera
tank	1	tank, cylinder, wheel, engine, steel acid, carbon, product, use, zinc	industry, export, industrial, economy, company network, user, server, datum, protocol
	2	army, force, infantry, military, battle however, attempt, result, despite, fail	aircraft, navy, missile, ship, flight war, german, ii, germany, world
race	1	win, world, cup, play, championship	two, one, three, four, another
	2	railway, line, train, road, rail	car, company, sell, manufacturer, model
	3	population, language, ethnic, native, people	female, age, woman, male, household
run	1	system, architecture, develop, base, language	access, need, require, allow, program
	2	railway, line, train, road, rail	also, well, several, early, see
	3	game, team, season, win, league	game, player, run, deal, baseball
tablet	1	bc, source, greek, ancient, date	book, publish, write, work, edition
	2	use, system, design, term, method	version, game, release, original, file
	3	system, blood, vessel, artery, intestine	patient, symptom, treatment, disorder, may

Table 1: Examples of sense clusters on polysemous words. When the number of clusters is set to be 2, we present the top 4 basis indexes b_j in each sense cluster, which have the highest values on the target word embedding $\mathbf{w}_q[b_j]$. Otherwise, the top 2 basis indexes are presented. CID refers to sense cluster ID. The top 5 words with the highest values of each basis index $\mathbf{w}[b_j]$ are presented.

senses of the target word with maximal similarity (i.e., $SIM(w_q, \mathbf{e}_c) = \max_k \cos(\mathbf{s}_k^q, \mathbf{e}_c)$). Then, we rank the similarity of 11 query pairs, which consist of 1 true context and 10 false contexts. The performance of different methods is evaluated by checking whether the top 1 (i.e., the pair with the highest similarity) is true. The metric (Sun et al., 2017) is called Precision@1.

The results are shown in Table 2. Since the task is to identify the related contexts, skip-gram is a good baseline (Sun et al., 2017). In this dataset, each sense is equally important, regardless how often the sense appears in the corpus. The significantly better performance from DIVE demonstrates our capability of modeling more fine-grained senses of polysemous words.

4.3 TWSI Evaluation

The Turk bootstrap Word Sense Inventory (TWSI) task (Biemann, 2012) is based on a large dataset,

Skip-gram	WG	WG+EM
52.7	42.1	59.1
MSSG	DIVE (100)	DIVE (300)
60	**63.2**	62.6

Table 2: Precision@1 on the WCR R1 (%).

which consists of 1,012 nouns accompanied with 145,140 context sentences. The task is to identify the correct sense of the target nouns, and all WSI algorithms choose the sense whose embedding is most similar to the context embedding.

Dataset is heavily skewed with 79% of contexts being assigned to the most frequent senses. To remove this bias, we follow the procedure described in Pelevina et al. (2016) to create balanced TWSI. Specifically, we only keep the first 5 contexts of each sense of every target word to make every sense count equally. The procedure yields 8710 pairs of senses and contexts.

Model	TWSI			balanced TWSI		
	P	R	F1	P	R	F1
MSSG rnd	66.1	65.7	65.9	33.9	33.7	33.8
MSSG	66.2	65.8	66.0	34.3	34.2	34.2
WG	**68.6**	**68.1**	**68.4**	38.7	38.5	38.6
WG+EM	68.3	67.8	68.0	38.4	38.2	38.3
DIVE rnd	63.4	63.0	63.2	33.4	33.2	33.3
DIVE (100)	67.6	67.2	67.4	**39.7**	**39.5**	**39.6**
DIVE (300)	67.4	66.9	67.2	39.0	38.8	38.9

Table 3: Results obtained on the TWSI task (%), where P is precision and R is recall. MSSG rnd and DIVE rnd are baselines which randomly assign sense given inventory built by MSSG and DIVE, respectively.

Model	JI	Tau	WNDCG	FNMI	FB-C
All-1	19.2	60.9	28.8	0	**62.3**
Rnd	21.8	62.8	28.7	2.8	47.4
MSSG	**22.2**	**62.9**	29.0	3.2	48.9
WG	21.2	61.2	29.0	1.6	58.1
WG+EM	21.0	61.5	29.0	1.3	57.8
DIVE (100)	21.9	61.9	**29.3**	3.1	50.6
DIVE (300)	22.1	62.8	29.1	**3.5**	49.9

Table 4: Results obtained on the SemEval 2013 task (%), where JI is Jaccard Index, FNMI is Fuzzy NMI, and FB-C is Fuzzy B-Cubed. All-1 is to assign all senses to be the same and Rnd is to randomly assign all senses to 2 groups.

When evaluating on TWSI, each method needs to represent the sense by a sparse bag-of-word context feature called sense inventory. The evaluation script[3] first maps each sense predicted by each algorithm to a ground truth sense. Then, the problem becomes a classification task, which can be evaluated by precision, recall, and F1.

In Table 3, we can see that DIVE performs slightly worse than WG (Pelevina et al., 2016) in full TWSI, but becomes slightly better in balanced TWSI. We suspect this is because our number of sense is 2 but the WG generates the output where the average number of senses is around 1.5, which might do better when a sense of each word occurs most of the time. Notice that the comparison in balanced TWSI is fair because the experiments in Pelevina et al. (2016) show that WG performs worse when increasing number of clusters. The results also suggest that a sufficient number of basis vectors seldom group two senses together (otherwise, increasing the resolution/dimension of DIVE should be helpful).

---

[3] https://github.com/tudarmstadt-lt/context-eval

4.4 SemEval-2013 task 13 Evaluation

SemEval-2013 task 13 (Jurgens and Klapaftis, 2013) provides a smaller dataset which consists of 50 words which include nouns, verbs, and adjectives. The context prediction is done in the same way as TWSI, and the meaning of each metric could be found in Jurgens and Klapaftis (2013). In Table 4, we can see our method performs roughly the same compared with other baselines.

5 Conclusions

We propose a novel graph-based WSI approach. In order to save the time of performing a nearest neighbor search, we first group words into basis/topics using distributional inclusion vector embedding (DIVE), compute target-dependent similarity between basis indexes, and then perform graph clustering. Our experimental results show that the method achieves the state-of-the-art performances and is able to capture less common senses with higher accuracy.

6 Acknowledgement

This material is based upon work supported in part by the Center for Data Science and the Center for Intelligent Information Retrieval, in part by Lexalytics, in part by the Chan Zuckerberg Initiative under the project Scientific Knowledge Base Construction, and in part by the National Science Foundation under Grant No. IIS-1514053 and No. DMR-1534431, in part using high performance computing equipment obtained under a grant from the Collaborative R&D Fund managed by the Massachusetts Technology Collaborative. Any opinions, findings and conclusions or recommendations expressed in this material are those of the authors and do not necessarily reflect those of the sponsor.

References

Eneko Agirre, David Martínez, Oier Lopez de Lacalle, and Aitor Soroa. 2006. Two graph-based algorithms for state-of-the-art WSD. In *EMNLP 2007, Proceedings of the 2006 Conference on Empirical Methods in Natural Language Processing, 22-23 July 2006, Sydney, Australia*.

Sanjeev Arora, Yuanzhi Li, Yingyu Liang, Tengyu Ma, and Andrej Risteski. 2016. Linear algebraic structure of word senses, with applications to polysemy. *arXiv preprint arXiv:1601.03764* .

Ben Athiwaratkun and Andrew Gordon Wilson. 2017. Multimodal word distributions. In *ACL*.

Marco Baroni, Silvia Bernardini, Adriano Ferraresi, and Eros Zanchetta. 2009. The WaCky wide web: a collection of very large linguistically processed web-crawled corpora. *Language resources and evaluation* 43(3):209–226.

Sergey Bartunov, Dmitry Kondrashkin, Anton Osokin, and Dmitry P. Vetrov. 2016. Breaking sticks and ambiguities with adaptive skip-gram. In *Proceedings of the 19th International Conference on Artificial Intelligence and Statistics, AISTATS 2016, Cadiz, Spain, May 9-11, 2016*.

Chris Biemann. 2006. Chinese whispers: an efficient graph clustering algorithm and its application to natural language processing problems. In *Proceedings of the first workshop on graph based methods for natural language processing*.

Chris Biemann. 2012. Turk bootstrap word sense inventory 2.0: A large-scale resource for lexical substitution. In *Proceedings of the Eighth International Conference on Language Resources and Evaluation, LREC 2012, Istanbul, Turkey, May 23-25, 2012*.

Haw-Shiuan Chang, ZiYun Wang, Luke Vilnis, and Andrew McCallum. 2018. Distributional inclusion vector embedding for unsupervised hypernymy detection. In *Human Language Technology Conference of the North American Chapter of the Association of Computational Linguistics (HLT/NAACL)*.

Antonio Di Marco and Roberto Navigli. 2013. Clustering and diversifying web search results with graph-based word sense induction. *Computational Linguistics* 39(3):709–754.

Beate Dorow and Dominic Widdows. 2003. Discovering corpus-specific word senses. In *EACL 2003, 10th Conference of the European Chapter of the Association for Computational Linguistics, April 12-17, 2003, Agro Hotel, Budapest, Hungary*.

David Hope and Bill Keller. 2013. Maxmax: a graph-based soft clustering algorithm applied to word sense induction. In *International Conference on Intelligent Text Processing and Computational Linguistics*.

David Jurgens and Ioannis Klapaftis. 2013. Semeval-2013 task 13: Word sense induction for graded and non-graded senses. In *Second Joint Conference on Lexical and Computational Semantics (* SEM), Volume 2: Proceedings of the Seventh International Workshop on Semantic Evaluation (SemEval 2013)*.

Jey Han Lau, Paul Cook, Diana McCarthy, David Newman, and Timothy Baldwin. 2012. Word sense induction for novel sense detection. In *EACL 2012, 13th Conference of the European Chapter of the Association for Computational Linguistics, Avignon, France, April 23-27, 2012*.

Omer Levy, Yoav Goldberg, and Ido Dagan. 2015. Improving distributional similarity with lessons learned from word embeddings. *Transactions of the Association for Computational Linguistics* 3:211–225.

Jiwei Li and Dan Jurafsky. 2015. Do multi-sense embeddings improve natural language understanding? In *Proceedings of the 2015 Conference on Empirical Methods in Natural Language Processing, EMNLP 2015, Lisbon, Portugal, September 17-21, 2015*.

Dekang Lin et al. 1998. An information-theoretic definition of similarity. In *ICML*.

Binny Mathew, Suman Kalyan Maity, Pratip Sarkar, Animesh Mukherjee, and Pawan Goyal. 2017. Adapting predominant and novel sense discovery algorithms for identifying corpus-specific sense differences. In *Proceedings of TextGraphs@ACL 2017: the 11th Workshop on Graph-based Methods for Natural Language Processing, Vancouver, Canada, August 3, 2017*.

Tomas Mikolov, Ilya Sutskever, Kai Chen, Greg S Corrado, and Jeff Dean. 2013. Distributed representations of words and phrases and their compositionality. In *NIPS*.

George A. Miller. 1995. Wordnet: a lexical database for english. *Communications of the ACM* 38(11):39–41.

Sunny Mitra, Ritwik Mitra, Martin Riedl, Chris Biemann, Animesh Mukherjee, and Pawan Goyal. 2014. That's sick dude!: Automatic identification of word sense change across different timescales. In *Proceedings of the 52nd Annual Meeting of the Association for Computational Linguistics, ACL 2014, June 22-27, 2014, Baltimore, MD, USA, Volume 1: Long Papers*.

Jiaqi Mu, Suma Bhat, and Pramod Viswanath. 2017. Geometry of polysemy. In *ICLR*.

Roberto Navigli and Giuseppe Crisafulli. 2010. Inducing word senses to improve web search result clustering. In *Proceedings of the 2010 conference on empirical methods in natural language processing*.

Arvind Neelakantan, Jeevan Shankar, Alexandre Passos, and Andrew McCallum. 2014. Efficient non-parametric estimation of multiple embeddings per word in vector space. In *Proceedings of the 2014 Conference on Empirical Methods in Natural Language Processing, EMNLP 2014, October 25-29, 2014, Doha, Qatar, A meeting of SIGDAT, a Special Interest Group of the ACL*.

Patrick Pantel and Dekang Lin. 2002. Discovering word senses from text. In *Proceedings of the eighth ACM SIGKDD international conference on Knowledge discovery and data mining*.

F. Pedregosa, G. Varoquaux, A. Gramfort, V. Michel, B. Thirion, O. Grisel, M. Blondel, P. Prettenhofer, R. Weiss, V. Dubourg, J. Vanderplas, A. Passos, D. Cournapeau, M. Brucher, M. Perrot, and

E. Duchesnay. 2011. Scikit-learn: Machine learning in Python. *Journal of Machine Learning Research* 12(Oct):2825–2830.

Maria Pelevina, Nikolay Arefiev, Chris Biemann, and Alexander Panchenko. 2016. Making sense of word embeddings. In *Proceedings of the 1st Workshop on Representation Learning for NLP, Rep4NLP@ACL 2016, Berlin, Germany, August 11, 2016.*

Luis Nieto Piña and Richard Johansson. 2015. A simple and efficient method to generate word sense representations. In *Recent Advances in Natural Language Processing, RANLP 2015, 7-9 September, 2015, Hissar, Bulgaria.*

Joseph Reisinger and Raymond J. Mooney. 2010. Multi-prototype vector-space models of word meaning. In *Human Language Technologies: Conference of the North American Chapter of the Association of Computational Linguistics, Proceedings, June 2-4, 2010, Los Angeles, California, USA.*

Hinrich Schütze. 1992. Dimensions of meaning. In *Proceedings of the 1992 ACM/IEEE conference on Supercomputing.*

X Yu Stella and Jianbo Shi. 2003. Multiclass spectral clustering. In *ICCV.*

Chiraag Sumanth and Diana Inkpen. 2015. How much does word sense disambiguation help in sentiment analysis of micropost data? In *Proceedings of the 6th Workshop on Computational Approaches to Subjectivity, Sentiment and Social Media Analysis.*

Yifan Sun, Nikhil Rao, and Weicong Ding. 2017. A simple approach to learn polysemous word embeddings. *arXiv preprint arXiv:1707.01793 .*

Fei Tian, Hanjun Dai, Jiang Bian, Bin Gao, Rui Zhang, Enhong Chen, and Tie-Yan Liu. 2014. A probabilistic model for learning multi-prototype word embeddings. In *COLING.*

Jean Véronis. 2004. Hyperlex: lexical cartography for information retrieval. *Computer Speech & Language* 18(3):223–252.

Fusing Document, Collection and Label Graph-based Representations with Word Embeddings for Text Classification

Konstantinos Skianis
École Polytechnique
France
kskianis@lix.polytechnique.fr

Fragkiskos D. Malliaros
CentraleSupélec and Inria Saclay
France
fragkiskos.me@gmail.com

Michalis Vazirgiannis
École Polytechnique
France
mvazirg@lix.polytechnique.fr

Abstract

Contrary to the traditional *Bag-of-Words* approach, we consider the *Graph-of-Words* (GoW) model in which each document is represented by a graph that encodes relationships between the different terms. Based on this formulation, the importance of a term is determined by weighting the corresponding node in the document, collection and label graphs, using node centrality criteria. We also introduce novel graph-based weighting schemes by enriching graphs with word-embedding similarities, in order to reward or penalize semantic relationships. Our methods produce more discriminative feature weights for text categorization, outperforming existing frequency-based criteria. Code and data are available online[1].

1 Introduction

With the rapid growth of the social media and networking platforms, the available textual resources have been increased. *Text categorization* or classification (TC) refers to the supervised learning task of assigning a document to a set of two or more predefined categories (or classes) (Sebastiani, 2002). Well-known applications of TC include sentiment analysis, spam detection and news classification.

In the TC pipeline, each document is modeled using the so-called *Vector Space Model* (Baeza-Yates and Ribeiro-Neto, 1999). The main issue here is how to find appropriate weights regarding the importance of each term in a document. Typically, the *Bag-of-Words* (BoW) model is applied and a document is represented as a multiset of its terms, disregarding co-occurence between

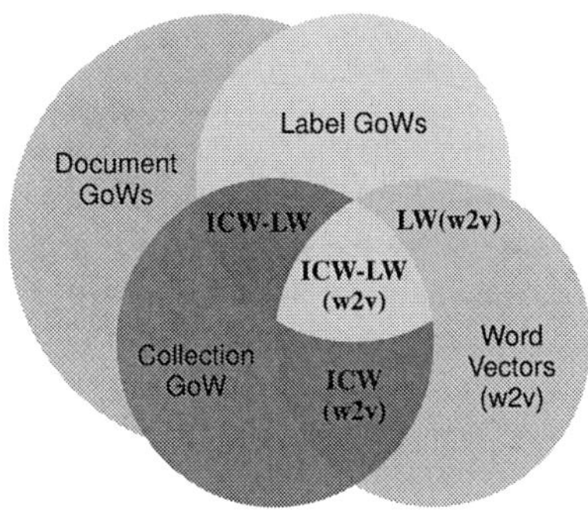

Figure 1: Blending different types of GoWs and word vector similarities in one framework.

the terms; using this model, the importance of a term in a document is mainly determined by the frequency of the term. Although several variants and extensions of this modeling approach have been proposed (e.g., the n-gram model (Baeza-Yates and Ribeiro-Neto, 1999)), the main weakness comes from the underlying term independence assumption, where the order of the terms is also completely disregarded.

After the introduction of deep learning models for TC (Blunsom et al., 2014; Kim, 2014), recent work by Johnson and Zhang (2015) shows how we could effectively use the order of words with CNNs (LeCun et al., 1995). In many cases though, space and time limitations may arise due to complex neural network architectures. As stated in work by Joulin et al. (2017), computation can still be expensive and prohibitive.

In this paper, we explore fast term weighting criteria for TC that go beyond the term independence assumption. The notion of dependencies between terms is introduced via a *Graph-of-Words* (GoW) representation model. Under this model, each term is represented as a node in the graph and the edges capture co-occurrence relationships

---

[1]Code and data: github.com/y3nk0/Graph-Based-TC

49

Proceedings of the Twelfth Workshop on Graph-Based Methods for Natural Language Processing (TextGraphs-12), pages 49–58
New Orleans, Louisiana, June 6, 2018. ©2018 Association for Computational Linguistics

of terms with a specified distance in the document. We implicitly consider information about n-grams in the document as well as the collection of documents – expressed by paths in the graph – without increasing the dimensionality of the problem. Furthermore, we introduce word-embedding similarities as weights in the GoW approach, in order to further boost the performance of our methods. Finally, we successfully mix document, collection and label GoWs along with word vector similarities into a single powerful graph-based framework. An overview of our approach is shown in Fig. 1.

2 Related Work

Term weighting schemes. A core aspect in the *Vector Space Model* for document representation, is how to determine the importance of a term within a document. Many criteria have been introduced with the most prominent ones being TF, TF-IDF (Salton and Buckley, 1988; Singhal et al., 1996; Baeza-Yates and Ribeiro-Neto, 1999; Robertson, 2004) and Okapi BM25 (Robertson et al., 1995), while some recent ones include N-gram IDF (Shirakawa et al., 2015). Lan et al. (2005) conducted a comparative study of frequency-based term weighting criteria for text categorization; one of their outcomes was that, in many cases, the IDF factor is not significant for the categorization task, leading to no improvement of the performance. It is interesting to point out here that, more specialized approaches have been proposed for specific classification tasks, such as the Delta TF-IDF method that constitutes an extension of TF-IDF for sentiment analysis (Martineau and Finin, 2009). However, most of the previously proposed frequency-based weights consider the document as a *Bag-of-Words*; that way, any structural information about the ordering or in general, syntactic relationship of the terms, is ignored by the weighting process.

Text categorization. A number of diverse approaches have been proposed for TC (Joachims, 1998; McCallum and Nigam, 1998; Nigam et al., 2000; Sebastiani, 2002; Kim et al., 2006). The first step of TC concerns the feature extraction task, i.e., which features will be used to represent the textual content. Typically, the straightforward *Bag-of-Words* approach is adopted, where every document is represented by a feature vector that contains boolean or weighted representation of unigrams or n-grams in general. In the case

of weighted feature vectors, various term weighting schemes have been used, with the most well-known ones being TF (Term Frequency), TF-IDF (Term Frequency - Inverse Document Frequency). Although these weighting schemes were initially introduced in the NLP and IR fields, they have also been applied in the TC task. Paltoglou and Thelwall (2010) reported that, in the case of sentiment analysis, extensions of the TF-IDF weighting schemes introduced in the IR field, can further improve the classification accuracy. A comprehensive review of this area is offered in the article by Sebastiani (2002).

Deep Learning for TC. With the rise of deep learning models, CNNs were applied for text classification (Blunsom et al., 2014; Kim, 2014; Johnson and Zhang, 2015). Next, Zhang et al. (2015) presented Character-level CNNs for the task of TC. Finally, Joulin et al. (2017) proposed a novel text classifier which achieves equivalent performance to state-of-the-art TC models, with faster learning times. Our work does not focus on the classifier part, as the aforementioned methods, but on the extraction of better features.

Graph-based text categorization. In the related literature, most of the graph-based method for TC, rely on graph mining algorithms that are applied to extract frequent subgraphs, which are then used to produce feature vectors for classification (Deshpande et al., 2005; Jiang et al., 2010; Rousseau et al., 2015; Nikolentzos et al., 2017). The basic shortcoming of those methods stems from the computational complexity of the frequent subgraph mining algorithm. Furthermore, most of these methods require from the user to set the *support* parameter, which concerns the frequency of appearance of a subgraph. Close to our work are the approaches followed by Hassan et al. (2007) and Malliaros and Skianis (2015); they explored how random walks and other graph centrality criteria can be applied to determine the importance of a term.

Graph-based text mining, NLP and IR. Representing documents as graphs is a well-known approach in NLP and IR. TextRank algorithm, proposed by Mihalcea and Tarau (2004), was among the first works that considered a random walk model similar to PageRank, over a graph representation of the document, in order to extract representative keywords and sentences. Later, sev-

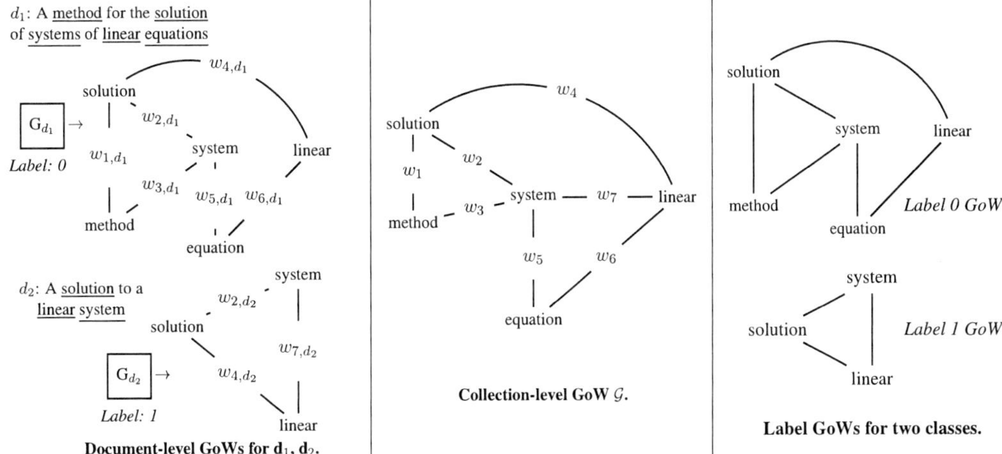

Figure 2: Example of document, collection-level and label GoWs for a collection composed by two documents and window size $w = 3$. Weights on the edges of G_{d_1} and G_{d_2} correspond to the similarity of two terms in the vector space. Here, Label GoWs are the same with Document GoWs (one document per class-label).

eral methods for those tasks were followed (Erkan and Radev, 2004; Litvak and Last, 2008; Boudin, 2013; Lahiri et al., 2014; Rousseau and Vazirgiannis, 2015). Another domain where graph-based term weighting schemes have been applied is the one of ad hoc Information Retrieval (Rousseau and Vazirgiannis, 2013). An interesting survey can be found in the work of Blanco and Lioma (2012) for a detailed description of graph-based methods in the text domain.

3 Preliminaries and Background

Let $\mathcal{D} = \{d_1, d_2, \ldots, d_m\}$ be a collection of documents and let $\mathcal{C} = \{c_1, c_2, \ldots, c_{|\mathcal{C}|}\}$ be the set of predefined categories. Text categorization is considered the task of assigning a boolean value to each pair $(d_i, c_i) \in \mathcal{D} \times \mathcal{C}$, i.e., assigning each document to one or more categories (Sebastiani, 2002). The main point here is how to find appropriate *weights* for the terms within a document. As we will present below shortly, our approach utilizes network centrality criteria.

Node Centrality Criteria. Centrality[2] represents a central notion in graph theory and network analysis in general; it constitutes of measures that capture the relative importance of the node in the graph based on specific criteria (Newman, 2010). One important characteristic of the centrality measures is that they consider either *local* information

of the graph (e.g., degree centrality, in-degree/out-degree centrality in directed networks, weighted degree in weighted graphs, clustering coefficient) (Newman, 2010), or more *global* information – in the sense that the importance of a node is determined by the properties of the node globally in the graph (e.g., PageRank, closeness). Let $G = (V, E)$ be a graph (directed or undirected), and let $|V|, |E|$ be the number of nodes and edges respectively. Next, we define basic centrality criteria that are used in the proposed methodology.

Degree centrality. The degree centrality is one of the simplest local node importance criteria, which captures the number of neighbors that each node has. Let $\mathcal{N}(i)$ be the set of nodes connected to node i. Then, the degree centrality can be derived based on the following formula: degree_centrality$(i) = \frac{|\mathcal{N}(i)|}{|V|-1}$.

Closeness centrality. Let $dist(i, j)$ be the shortest path distance between nodes i and j. The closeness centrality of a node i is defined as the inverse of the average shortest path distance from the node to any other node in the graph: closeness$(i) = \frac{|V|-1}{\sum_{j \in V} dist(i,j)}$.

PageRank centrality. PageRank counts the number and quality of edges to a node to determine a rough estimate of how important the node is: $PR(i) = \frac{1-\alpha}{|V|} + \alpha \sum_{\forall (j,i) \in E} \frac{PR(j)}{\text{out-deg}(j)}$, where α is the teleportation probability and out-deg(i) denotes the out degree on node i.

[2]en.wikipedia.org/wiki/Centrality.

4 Proposed Framework

In this section, we present the components of the proposed graph-based framework for TC.

4.1 Graph Construction

We model documents as graphs that capture dependencies between terms. More precisely, each document $d \in \mathcal{D}$ is represented by a graph $G_d = (V_d, E_d)$, where the nodes correspond to the terms t of the document and the edges capture co-occurrence relationships between terms within a fixed-size sliding window of size w. That is, for all the terms that co-occur within the window, we add edges between the corresponding nodes of the graph. Note that, the windows are overlapping starting from the first term of the document; at each step, we simply remove the first term of the window and add the new one from the document. As graphs constitute rich modeling structures, several parameters about the construction phase need to be specified, including the directionality of the edges, the addition of edge weights, well as the size w of the sliding window. Fig. 2 gives a toy example of the construction of GoW for a collection composed by two documents.

To summarize, the key point of the graph-based representation for TC is the fact that it deals with the term independence assumption. Even if we consider the n-gram model, still information about the relationship between two different n-grams is not fully captured – as happens in the case of graphs. This has also been noted in other application domains (e.g., IR (Rousseau and Vazirgiannis, 2013)).

4.2 Term Weighting

Having the graph, the importance of a term in a document can be inferred by the importance of the corresponding node in the graph. In the previous section, we presented local and global centrality criteria that have been widely used for graph mining and network analysis purposes; here, we propose that those criteria can also be used for weighting terms in the TC task. That way, similar to TF, we can define the Term Weight (TW) weighting scheme as $\mathrm{TW}(t, d) = \mathrm{centrality}(t, d)$, where $\mathrm{centrality}(t, d)$ corresponds to the score of term (node) t in the graph representation G_d of document d. The interesting point here is that TW can be used along with any centrality criterion in the graph, local or global.

Furthermore, we can extend this weighting scheme by considering information about the inverse document frequency (IDF factor) of the term t in the collection $\mathcal{D}$. That way, we can derive the TW-IDF model as follows:

$$\mathrm{TW\text{-}IDF}(t, d) = \mathrm{TW}(t, d) \times \mathrm{IDF}(t, \mathcal{D}). \quad (1)$$

In fact, TW and TW-IDF constitute suites for graph-based term-weighting schemes and thus, can be applied in any text analytics task. Some of them have already been explored in graph-based IR (Rousseau and Vazirgiannis, 2013) and keyword extraction (Mihalcea and Tarau, 2004; Rousseau and Vazirgiannis, 2015).

The proposed weights are inferred from the interconnection of features (i.e., terms) – as suggested by the graph – and therefore information about n-grams is implicitly captured. That way, the feature space of the learning problem is kept to the one defined by the unique unigrams of our collection (instead of using simultaneously as features all the possible unigrams, bigrams, 3-grams, etc.), but the produced term weights incorporate n-gram information through the graph-based representation.

4.3 Inverse Collection Weight (ICW)

In this paragraph, we introduce the concept of *Inverse Collection Weight* (ICW) – a graph-based criterion to penalize the weight of terms that are "important" across the whole collection of documents. The main concept behind ICW is the *collection level* graph $\mathcal{G}$ – an extension of the *Graph-of-Words* in the collection of documents $\mathcal{D}$.

Definition 1 (Collection Level Graph $\mathcal{G}$) *Let $\{G_1, G_2, \ldots, G_d\}_{|\mathcal{D}|}$ be the set of graphs that correspond to all documents $d \in \mathcal{D}$. The collection level graph $\mathcal{G}$ is defined as the union of graphs $G_1 \cup G_2 \cup \ldots \cup G_d$ over all documents in the collection.*

The union of two graphs $G = (V_G, E_G)$ and $H = (V_H, E_H)$ is defined as the union of their node and edge sets, i.e., $G \cup H = (V_G \cup V_H, E_G \cup E_H)$. The number of nodes in graph $\mathcal{G}$ is equal to the number of unique terms in the collection, while the number of edges is equal to the number of unique edges over all document-level graphs (see also Fig. 2).

This graph captures the overall dependencies between the terms of the collection; the relative overall importance of a term in the collection will be proportional to the importance of the corresponding node in $\mathcal{G}$. Following similar methodological arguments as used for IDF (Robertson, 2004), we define a probability distribution over the nodes of $\mathcal{G}$ (or equivalently, the unique terms of $\mathcal{D}$), with respect to a centrality (term-weighting in our case) criterion; then, the probability of node (term) t will be:

$$\Pr(t) = \frac{\mathrm{TW}(t, \mathcal{D})}{\sum_{v \in \mathcal{D}} \mathrm{TW}(v, \mathcal{D})}. \tag{2}$$

Note that, in Eq. (2), we use $\mathcal{D}$ instead of $\mathcal{G}$; we consider that the space defined by the document collection $\mathcal{D}$ is equivalent to the one defined by graph $\mathcal{G}$ with respect to the unique terms of the collection. This way, the notion of $\mathrm{TW}(t, \mathcal{D})$ used here is consistent with what was described earlier. Based on this, we define the ICW measure as:

$$\mathrm{ICW}(t, \mathcal{D}) = \frac{\max_{v \in \mathcal{D}} \mathrm{TW}(v, \mathcal{D})}{\mathrm{TW}(t, \mathcal{D})}. \tag{3}$$

Instead of selecting the *maximum* centrality in the collection level (Eq. (3)), the *sum* of all centralities also yields good results.

ICW shares common intuition with the *inverse total term frequency* described in Robertson (2004). In fact, it can be considered as an extension of the total collection frequency of a term, to the graph-based document representation. Furthermore, similar to TW, it can be used along with any node centrality criterion.

Using ICW as a graph-based collection-level term penalization factor, we derive a new class of term-to-document weighting mechanism, namely TW-ICW. This weighting scheme is derived combining different local (i.e., document-level) and global (i.e., collection-level) criteria as follows:

$$\mathrm{TW\text{-}ICW}(t, d) = \mathrm{TW}(t, d) \times \log(\mathrm{ICW}(t, \mathcal{D})).$$

In the case of TW and ICW, any centrality criterion can be applied. However, the computational complexity is a crucial factor that should be taken into account. Nevertheless, as we have noticed from the experimental evaluation, even using simple and easy-to-compute local criteria (e.g., degree), we achieve good classification performance.

4.4 Label Graphs

Shanavas et al. (2016) introduced supervised term weighting (TW-CRC) as a method to integrate class information with graphs. Similarly, we create a graph for each class (label), where we add all words of documents belonging to the respective class as nodes and their co-occurrence as edges. Our weighting scheme is a variant of TW-CRC; we define LW for a term t as:

$$\mathrm{LW}(t) = \frac{\max(\deg(t, L))}{\max(\mathrm{avg}(\deg(t, L)), \min(\deg(L)))},$$

where the maximum degree of term t in all label graphs (L) is divided by the max of two values: the average degree of the term in all label graphs (except the one having the max degree) and the min degree of all the terms in all the label graphs. Then, we obtain ICW-LW as follows:

$$\mathrm{ICW\text{-}LW}(t, d) = \log(\mathrm{ICW}(t, \mathcal{D}) \times \mathrm{LW}(t)),$$

and multiply it with $\mathrm{TW}(t, d)$ to get TW-ICW-LW. Notice that, supervised frequency-based methods have also been proposed in previous work (Debole and Sebastiani, 2004; Huynh et al., 2011).

4.5 Edge Weighting using Word Embeddings

With our proposed framework, we can now use word embeddings (Bengio et al., 2003) in order to extract similarities between terms. Our goal is to integrate these similarities in the graph representation as weights on the edge between two words. The key idea behind our approach is that we want to reward semantically close words in the graph-document level (TW) and penalize them in the collection level (ICW).

The most commonly used similarity between two words t_1 and t_2 in the word-embedding space is cosine similarity, which ranges between -1 and 1. In order to have a valid distance metric, we need to bound this between 0 and 1. We use the angular similarity to represent the weight of an edge between two words, and since the vector elements may be positive or negative, the formula becomes:

$$\mathrm{weight}(t_1, t_2) = 1 - \frac{\arccos(\mathrm{sim}(t_1, t_2))}{\pi}. \tag{4}$$

The best performance was given by using Google's pre-trained word embeddings (Mikolov et al., 2013) and not by learning them by the datasets. Since the words included in the pre-trained version of word2vec are case sensitive and not stemmed, we did not apply any of these transformations. For words that do not appear in word2vec, we add a small value as similarity. Other distances (e.g. inverse euclidean, fractional) did not yield any further improvement.

Table 1: Datasets' statistics: #ICW shows the number of edges in the collection-level graph; #w2v: number of words that exist in pre-trained vectors.

	Train	Test	Voc	Avg	#w2v	#ICW
IMDB	1,340	660	32,844	343	27,462	352K
WEBKB	2,803	1,396	23,206	179	20,990	273K
20NG	11,293	7,528	62,752	155	54,892	1.7M
AMAZON	5,359	2,640	19,980	65	19,646	274K
REUTERS	5,485	2,189	11,965	66	9,218	163K
SUBJ.	6,694	3,293	8,639	11	8,097	58K

A similar approach for generic *keyphrase extraction* can be tracked in work by Wang et al. (2015). Providing more information in the weights, like number of co-occurrences between words, did not yield better results.

4.6 Classification Algorithms

Since the goal of this paper is to introduce new term weighting schemes, we rely on widely used classification algorithms. Specifically, we have used linear SVMs, due to their superior performance in TC (Joachims, 1998). Furthermore, as discussed in Leopold and Kindermann (2002), the choice of the kernel function of SVM is not very crucial, compared to the significance of the term weighting schemes.

5 Experiments

We have evaluated our method on six freely available standard TC datasets, covering multi-class document categorization, sentiment analysis and subjectivity. Specifically: (1) 20NG[3]: newsgroup documents belonging to 20 categories, (2) REUTERS[3]: 8 categories of Reuters-21578, (3) WEBKB[3]: 4 most frequent categories of webpages from Computer Science departments, (4) IMDB (Pang and Lee, 2004): positive and negative movie reviews; (5) AMAZON (Blitzer et al., 2007): product reviews acquired from Amazon over four different sub-collections; (6) SUBJECTIVITY (Pang and Lee, 2004): contains subjective sentences gathered from Rotten Tomatoes and objective sentences gathered from IMDB. A summary of the datasets can be found in Table 1.

In the experiments, linear SVMs were used with grid search cross-validation for tuning the C parameter. We also examined logistic regression, and observed similar performance. In the text

---

[3]web.ist.utl.pt/acardoso/datasets/

preprocessing step, we have removed stopwords. No stemming or lowercase transformation was applied in order to match the words in word2vec.

For evaluation we use macro-average F1 score and classification accuracy on the test sets; that way, we deal with the skewed class size distribution of some datasets (Sebastiani, 2002). For the notation of the proposed schemes, we use TW (centrality measure) (e.g., TW (degree)) to indicate the centrality and TW-ICW (centrality at G, centrality at $\mathcal{G}$) (e.g., TW-ICW (degree, degree)) for the local and collection-level graphs respectively. In TW-IDF (w2v), we compute the weighted degree centrality on the document level, with word-embedding similarities as weights. Similarly, in TW-ICW (w2v) we compute both weighted centralities for document and collection graphs. Finally, we denote as TW-ICW-LW the blending of TW, ICW and label graphs (LW). In label graphs we only make use of the degree centrality, since it is fast and performs best.

5.1 Results

Table 2 presents the results concerning the categorization performance of the proposed schemes for the six datasets. As discussed previously, the size of the window considered to create the graphs is one of the model's parameters. From the extensive experimental evaluation that we have performed, we have concluded that small window sizes give the most persistent results across various datasets and weighting schemes. For completeness in the presentation, we report results for two window sizes. In order to capture more information, we need larger window sizes for small datasets (e.g. SUBJECTIVITY). Also, since for the baseline methods (TF, TF binary, TF-IDF, w2v, TF-IDF-w2v) there is no notion of window size, the results for $w = \{2, 3\}$ are the same. We have also examined several centrality criteria (using both undirected and directed graphs); undirected giving better results.

Comparing TF to the graph-based ones, namely TW (degree), in almost all cases TW gives higher F1 and accuracy results. Similar observations can be made in the case where the IDF penalization is applied. In most of the datasets, the TW-IDF (degree) scheme performs quite well. The interesting point here, which is confirmed by the related literature (Lan et al., 2005), is that TF-IDF is in general inferior to TF in TC. However, when

Table 2: Macro-F1 and accuracy for window size w. Bold shows the best performance on each window size and blue the best overall on each dataset. * indicates statistical significance of improvement over TF at $p < 0.05$ using micro sign test. MAX and SUM state the best nominator for ICW in Eq. (3).

Methods	20NG (MAX)				IMDB (SUM)				SUBJECTIVITY (MAX)			
	$w = 3$		$w = 4$		$w = 2$		$w = 3$		$w = 6$		$w = 7$	
	F1	Acc	F1	Acc	F1	Acc	F1	Acc	F1	Acc	F1	Acc
TF	80.88	81.55	-		84.23	84.24	-		88.42	88.43	-	
w2v	74.43	75.75	-		82.57	82.57	-		87.67	87.67	-	
TF-binary (ngrams)	81.64	82.11*	-		83.02	83.03	-		87.51	87.51	-	
TW (degree)	82.37	83.00*	82.21	82.83*	84.82	84.84	84.67	84.69	88.33	88.33	89.00	89.00*
TW (w2v)	81.88	82.51*	82.21	82.87*	84.66	84.69	84.52	84.54	87.75	87.57	87.66	87.67
TF-IDF	82.44	83.01*	-		83.33	83.33	-		89.06	89.06*	-	
TF-IDF-w2v	82.52	83.09*	-		82.87	82.87	-		89.91	89.91*	-	
TW-IDF (degree)	84.75	85.47*	84.80	85.46*	82.86	82.87	83.02	83.03	89.33	89.34*	89.33	89.34*
TW-IDF (w2v)	84.66	85.32	84.46	85.13	83.47	83.48	83.31	83.33	86.42	86.42	86.51	86.51
TW-ICW (deg, deg)	85.24	85.80*	**85.41**	**86.05***	84.98	85.00	85.13	85.15	89.30	89.31*	89.61	89.61*
TW-ICW (w2v)	**85.33**	**85.93***	85.29	85.90*	85.12	85.15	84.82	84.84	89.61	89.61*	87.30	87.30
TW-ICW-LW (deg)	85.01	85.66*	85.02	85.66*	85.73	85.75	85.28	85.30	**90.12**	**90.13***	90.27	90.28*
TW-ICW-LW (w2v)	82.56	83.11*	82.24	82.81*	85.29	85.30	84.39	84.39	87.70	87.70	87.70	87.70
TW-ICW-LW (pgr)	83.92	84.66	83.80	84.54	84.97	85.00	85.73	85.75	86.60	86.60	86.45	86.45
TW-ICW-LW (cl)	84.61	85.22	84.71	85.27	**87.27**	**87.27***	**86.06**	**86.06**	89.97	89.97*	90.09	90.10*

Methods	AMAZON (MAX)				WEBKB (SUM)				REUTERS (MAX)			
	$w = 2$		$w = 3$		$w = 2$		$w = 3$		$w = 2$		$w = 3$	
	F1	Acc	F1	Acc	F1	Acc	F1	Acc	F1	Acc	F1	Acc
TF	80.68	80.68	-		90.31	91.91	-		91.51	96.34	-	
w2v	79.05	79.05	-		84.54	86.58	-		91.35	96.84	-	
TF-binary (ngrams)	79.84	79.84	-		91.22	92.85	-		86.33	95.34	-	
TW (degree)	80.07	80.07			91.69	92.64	91.45	92.49	93.58	97.53*	93.08	97.25*
TW (w2v)	80.07	80.07	79.54	79.54	91.70	92.64	91.00	92.06	93.09	97.35*	93.43	97.25*
TF-IDF	80.26	80.26	-		87.79	89.89	-		91.89	96.71	-	
TF-IDF-w2v	80.49	80.49	-		88.18	90.18	-		91.33	96.80	-	
TW-IDF (degree)	81.47	81.47*	81.55	81.55*	90.38	91.70	90.47	91.84	93.80	97.30*	93.13	97.35*
TW-IDF (w2v)	79.61	79.62	77.60	77.61	90.81	92.20	90.60	91.91	93.38	97.44*	**93.87**	**97.44***
TW-ICW (deg, deg)	82.08	82.08*	82.02	82.02*	91.72	92.78	91.42	92.49	92.91	97.35	93.59	97.39*
TW-ICW (w2v)	80.86	80.87*	78.82	78.82	91.58	92.64	91.84	92.85	93.57	97.30*	92.96	97.25
TW-ICW-LW (deg)	82.72	82.72*	82.91	82.91*	91.86	92.92	91.95	92.92	**93.88**	**97.53***	93.48	97.35*
TW-ICW-LW (w2v)	80.56	80.56	78.32	78.33	90.74	91.99	90.01	91.34	92.51	96.89	92.14	96.98
TW-ICW-LW (pgr)	82.23	82.23*	82.46	82.46*	91.18	92.20	92.23	93.07	93.38	97.35*	93.37	97.35*
TW-ICW-LW (cl)	**82.90**	**82.91***	83.02	83.03*	**92.72**	**93.57***	**92.86**	**93.57***	93.12	97.25	92.87	97.21

the IDF penalization factor is applied on the TW term-to-document weighting, a powerful mechanism is derived. In the case of purely graph-based schemes, we can observe that some of them produce very good classification results. In almost all cases, TW-ICW-LW (degree or closeness) achieve the best performance.

Significant improvement is observed by adding the w2v similarities as weights in the document, collection level and label graphs in almost all datasets. In fact, we have obtained better results in 20NG (TW-ICW (w2v)), WebKB (TW-ICW (w2v)) and Reuters (TW-IDF(w2v)), by boosting semantically close words in the document level and penalizing them in the collection level.

TF n-gram binary scheme (TF binary) has also been examined, i.e., all the possible n-grams of the collection with binary weights (up to 6-grams in our experiments). For comparison reasons, the size of the unigram feature space considered by our framework is equal to the unique terms in the collections and much smaller compared to the $n-$grams ones. Moreover, graph-based weighting is able to outperform TF (binary) in all datasets.

We clearly see that by fusing document, collection and label graphs we obtain the best results in almost in 5 out of 6 datasets. Label graphs information consist a powerful weighting method, when combined with our proposed collection level graph approach. Adding word2vec similarities as weights, when label graphs are used, does not improve the accuracy. This implies that important

	20NG	IMDB	SUBJ.	AMAZON	WEBKB	REUTERS
CNN (no w2v, 20 ep.) (Kim, 2014)	83.19	74.09	88.16	80.68	88.17	94.75
FastText (100 ep.) (Joulin et al., 2017)	79.70	84.70	88.60	79.50	92.60	97.00
TextRank (Mihalcea and Tarau, 2004)	82.56	83.33	84.78	80.49	92.27	97.35
Word Attraction (Wang et al., 2015)	61.24	70.75	86.60	78.29	79.46	91.34
TW-CRC (Shanavas et al., 2016)	85.35	85.15	89.28	81.13	92.71	97.39
TW-ICW-LW (ours)	**86.05**	**87.27**	**90.28**	**83.03**	**93.57**	**97.53**

Table 3: Comparison in accuracy(%) to state-of-the-art deep learning and graph-based approaches.

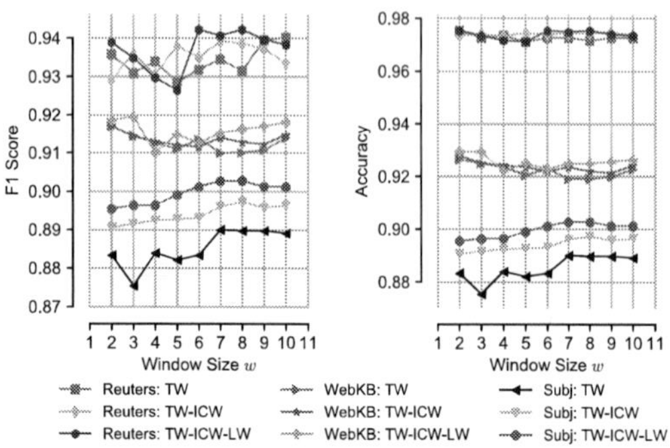

Figure 3: F1 score (left) and accuracy (right) of TW, TW-ICW and TW-ICW-LW (all degree) on REUTERS, WEBKB and SUBJECTIVITY, for window size $w = \{2, \ldots, 10\}$.

terms concerning different labels can be close in the word vector space. Choosing closeness in the document level GoW yields the best performance in 3 datasets. Closeness can only have an affect in larger document lengths and when used along with label graphs.

To further investigate the effectiveness of our approach, we have compared our results with current state-of-the-art graph-based and non graph-based methods. In Table 3 we compare against CNN for text classification ,without pre-trained word vectors (Kim, 2014), FastText (Joulin et al., 2017), TextRank (Mihalcea and Tarau, 2004), Word Attraction weights based on word2vec similarities (Wang et al., 2015) and Supervised Term Weighting (TW-CRC) by Shanavas et al. (2016). Our work produces comparable to state-of-the-art results. Since the implementation of most models is our own, their performance is not optimal.

Selecting the window size w is also important. As we observed, the maximum accuracy is achieved while using small window sizes. In any case, even if larger values of w were able to get slightly better results, a smaller window size would be preferable, due to the overall overhead

that could be introduced (increase of the density of the graph). Figure 3 depicts the F1 score and accuracy on the WEBKB, REUTERS and SUBJECTIVITY datasets, using the TW, TW-ICW and TW-ICW-LW(deg) schemes for various window sizes. We notice also that larger sliding windows are only improving accuracy in datasets with small document length (e.g. SUBJECTIVITY).

6   Conclusion & Future Work

In this paper, we proposed a graph-based framework for TC. By treating the term weighting task as a node ranking problem of interconnected features defined by a graph, we were able to determine the importance of a term using node centrality criteria. Building on this formulation, we introduced simple-yet-effective weighting schemes at the collection and label level, in order to penalize globally important terms (as analogous to "globally frequent terms") and reward locally important terms respectively. We also incorporate additional word-embedding information as weights in the graph-based representations.

Our proposed methods could also be applied in IR. In fact, document-level graph-based term weighting has already been applied there, so it would be interesting to examine the performance of the proposed collection-level (ICW) penalization mechanism. In the unsupervised scenario, where label information is not available, community detection algorithms may be applied to identify clusters of words or documents in collection graphs. Graph-based representations of text could also be fitted into deep learning architectures following the idea of Lei et al. (2015). Lastly, one could examine a *Graph-of-documents* approach, in which we create a graph, where nodes represent documents and edges correspond to similarity between them. In this case, graph kernels could be utilized for graph comparison and/or Word Mover's distance (Kusner et al., 2015) between two documents as weights.

References

Ricardo A. Baeza-Yates and Berthier Ribeiro-Neto. 1999. *Modern Information Retrieval*. Addison-Wesley Longman Publishing Co., Inc., Boston, MA, USA.

Yoshua Bengio, Réjean Ducharme, Pascal Vincent, and Christian Janvin. 2003. A neural probabilistic language model. *J. Mach. Learn. Res.* 3:1137–1155.

Roi Blanco and Christina Lioma. 2012. Graph-based term weighting for information retrieval. *Inf. Retr.* 15(1):54–92.

John Blitzer, Mark Dredze, and Fernando Pereira. 2007. Biographies, bollywood, boom-boxes and blenders: Domain adaptation for sentiment classification. In *Association for Computational Linguistics*. Prague, Czech Republic.

Phil Blunsom, Edward Grefenstette, and Nal Kalchbrenner. 2014. A convolutional neural network for modelling sentences. In *Proceedings of the 52nd Annual Meeting of the Association for Computational Linguistics*. Proceedings of the 52nd Annual Meeting of the Association for Computational Linguistics.

Florian Boudin. 2013. A comparison of centrality measures for graph-based keyphrase extraction. In *IJCNLP*. pages 834–838.

Franca Debole and Fabrizio Sebastiani. 2004. Supervised term weighting for automated text categorization. In *Text mining and its applications*, Springer, pages 81–97.

Mukund Deshpande, Michihiro Kuramochi, Nikil Wale, and George Karypis. 2005. Frequent substructure-based approaches for classifying chemical compounds. *IEEE Trans. on Knowl. and Data Eng.* 17(8):1036–1050.

Günes Erkan and Dragomir R. Radev. 2004. Lexrank: Graph-based lexical centrality as salience in text summarization. *J. Artif. Int. Res.* 22(1):457–479.

Samer Hassan, Rada Mihalcea, and Carmen Banea. 2007. Random-walk term weighting for improved text classification. In *ICSC*. pages 242–249.

Dat Huynh, Dat Tran, Wanli Ma, and Dharmendra Sharma. 2011. A new term ranking method based on relation extraction and graph model for text classification. In *Proceedings of the Thirty-Fourth Australasian Computer Science Conference-Volume 113*. Australian Computer Society, Inc., pages 145–152.

Chuntao Jiang, Frans Coenen, Robert Sanderson, and Michele Zito. 2010. Text classification using graph mining-based feature extraction. *Knowl.-Based Syst.* 23(4):302–308.

Thorsten Joachims. 1998. Text categorization with support vector machines: Learning with many relevant features. In *ECML*. pages 137–142.

Rie Johnson and Tong Zhang. 2015. Effective use of word order for text categorization with convolutional neural networks. In *NAACL HLT 2015, The 2015 Conference of the North American Chapter of the Association for Computational Linguistics: Human Language Technologies, Denver, Colorado, USA, May 31 - June 5, 2015*. pages 103–112.

Armand Joulin, Edouard Grave, Piotr Bojanowski, and Tomas Mikolov. 2017. Bag of tricks for efficient text classification. In *Proceedings of the 15th Conference of the European Chapter of the Association for Computational Linguistics*. pages 427–431.

Sang-Bum Kim, Kyoung-Soo Han, Hae-Chang Rim, and Sung-Hyon Myaeng. 2006. Some effective techniques for naive bayes text classification. *IEEE Trans. Knowl. Data Eng.* 18(11):1457–1466.

Yoon Kim. 2014. Convolutional neural networks for sentence classification. In *Proceedings of the 2014 Conference on Empirical Methods in Natural Language Processing*.

Matt Kusner, Yu Sun, Nicholas Kolkin, and Kilian Weinberger. 2015. From word embeddings to document distances. In *International Conference on Machine Learning*. pages 957–966.

Shibamouli Lahiri, Sagnik Ray Choudhury, and Cornelia Caragea. 2014. Keyword and keyphrase extraction using centrality measures on collocation networks. *CoRR* .

Man Lan, Chew-Lim Tan, Hwee-Boon Low, and Sam-Yuan Sung. 2005. A comprehensive comparative study on term weighting schemes for text categorization with support vector machines. In *WWW*. pages 1032–1033.

Yann LeCun, Yoshua Bengio, et al. 1995. Convolutional networks for images, speech, and time series. *The handbook of brain theory and neural networks* 3361(10):1995.

Tao Lei, Regina Barzilay, and Tommi Jaakkola. 2015. Molding cnns for text: non-linear, non-consecutive convolutions. *Proceedings of the 2015 Conference on Empirical Methods in Natural Language Processing* .

Edda Leopold and Jörg Kindermann. 2002. Text categorization with support vector machines. How to represent texts in input space? *Mach. Learn.* 46(1-3).

Marina Litvak and Mark Last. 2008. Graph-based keyword extraction for single-document summarization. In *MMIES*. pages 17–24.

Fragkiskos D. Malliaros and Konstantinos Skianis. 2015. Graph-based term weighting for text categorization. In *Proceedings of ASONAM*. pages 1473–1479.

Justin Martineau and Tim Finin. 2009. Delta tfidf: An improved feature space for sentiment analysis. In *ICWSM*.

Andrew McCallum and Kamal Nigam. 1998. A comparison of event models for naive bayes text classification. In *AAAI: Proceedings of the Workshop on Learning for Text Categorization*. pages 41–48.

Rada Mihalcea and Paul Tarau. 2004. Textrank: Bringing order into text. In *EMNLP*. pages 404–411.

Tomas Mikolov, Ilya Sutskever, Kai Chen, Greg S Corrado, and Jeff Dean. 2013. Distributed representations of words and phrases and their compositionality. In *Advances in neural information processing systems*. pages 3111–3119.

Mark Newman. 2010. *Networks: An Introduction*. Oxford University Press, Inc.

Kamal Nigam, Andrew Kachites McCallum, Sebastian Thrun, and Tom Mitchell. 2000. Text classification from labeled and unlabeled documents using EM. *Mach. Learn.* 39(2-3):103–134.

Giannis Nikolentzos, Polykarpos Meladianos, François Rousseau, Yannis Stavrakas, and Michalis Vazirgiannis. 2017. Shortest-path graph kernels for document similarity. In *Proceedings of the 2017 Conference on Empirical Methods in Natural Language Processing*. pages 1890–1900.

Georgios Paltoglou and Mike Thelwall. 2010. A study of information retrieval weighting schemes for sentiment analysis. In *ACL*. pages 1386–1395.

Bo Pang and Lillian Lee. 2004. A sentimental education: Sentiment analysis using subjectivity summarization based on minimum cuts. In *Proceedings of the ACL*.

Stephen Robertson. 2004. Understanding inverse document frequency: On theoretical arguments for idf. *Journal of Documentation* 60:2004.

Stephen E Robertson, Steve Walker, Susan Jones, Micheline M Hancock-Beaulieu, Mike Gatford, et al. 1995. Okapi at trec-3. *Nist Special Publication Sp* 109:109.

François Rousseau and Michalis Vazirgiannis. 2013. Graph-of-word and TW-IDF: new approach to ad hoc IR. In *CIKM*. pages 59–68.

François Rousseau and Michalis Vazirgiannis. 2015. Main core retention on graph-of-words for single-document keyword extraction. In *ECIR*. pages 382–393.

Franois Rousseau, Emmanouil Kiagias, and Michalis Vazirgiannis. 2015. Text categorization as a graph classification problem. In *ACL*.

Gerard Salton and Christopher Buckley. 1988. Term-weighting approaches in automatic text retrieval. *Inf. Process. Manage.* 24(5):513–523.

Fabrizio Sebastiani. 2002. Machine learning in automated text categorization. *ACM Comput. Surv.* 34(1):1–47.

Niloofer Shanavas, Hui Wang, Zhiwei Lin, and Glenn Hawe. 2016. Centrality-based approach for supervised term weighting. In *Data Mining Workshops (ICDMW), 2016 IEEE 16th International Conference on*. IEEE, pages 1261–1268.

Masumi Shirakawa, Takahiro Hara, and Shojiro Nishio. 2015. N-gram IDF: A global term weighting scheme based on information distance.

Amit Singhal, Chris Buckley, and Mandar Mitra. 1996. Pivoted document length normalization. In *SIGIR*. pages 21–29.

Rui Wang, Wei Liu, and Chris McDonald. 2015. Corpus-independent generic keyphrase extraction using word embedding vectors.

Xiang Zhang, Junbo Zhao, and Yann LeCun. 2015. Character-level convolutional networks for text classification. In *Advances in Neural Information Processing Systems 28*, Curran Associates, Inc., pages 649–657.

Embedding Text in Hyperbolic Spaces

Bhuwan Dhingra[*1]   **Christopher J. Shallue**[2]   **Mohammad Norouzi**[2]
Andrew M. Dai[2]   **George E. Dahl**[2]

[1]Carnegie Mellon University
[2]Google Brain
`bdhingra@cs.cmu.edu, {shallue, mnorouzi, adai, gdahl}@google.com`

Abstract

Natural language text exhibits hierarchical structure in a variety of respects. Ideally, we could incorporate our prior knowledge of this hierarchical structure into unsupervised learning algorithms that work on text data. Recent work by Nickel and Kiela (2017) proposed using hyperbolic instead of Euclidean embedding spaces to represent hierarchical data and demonstrated encouraging results when embedding graphs. In this work, we extend their method with a re-parameterization technique that allows us to learn hyperbolic embeddings of arbitrarily parameterized objects. We apply this framework to learn word and sentence embeddings in hyperbolic space in an unsupervised manner from text corpora. The resulting embeddings seem to encode certain intuitive notions of hierarchy, such as word-context frequency and phrase constituency. However, the implicit continuous hierarchy in the learned hyperbolic space makes interrogating the model's learned hierarchies more difficult than for models that learn explicit edges between items. The learned hyperbolic embeddings show improvements over Euclidean embeddings in some – but not all – downstream tasks, suggesting that hierarchical organization is more useful for some tasks than others.

1 Introduction

Many real-world datasets exhibit hierarchical structure, either explicitly in ontologies like Word-Net, or implicitly in social networks (Adcock et al., 2013) and natural language sentences (Everaert et al., 2015). When learning representations of such datasets, hyperbolic spaces have recently been advocated as alternatives to the standard Euclidean spaces in order to better represent the hierarchical structure (Nickel and Kiela, 2017; Cham-

---

*Work done while interning at Google Brain.

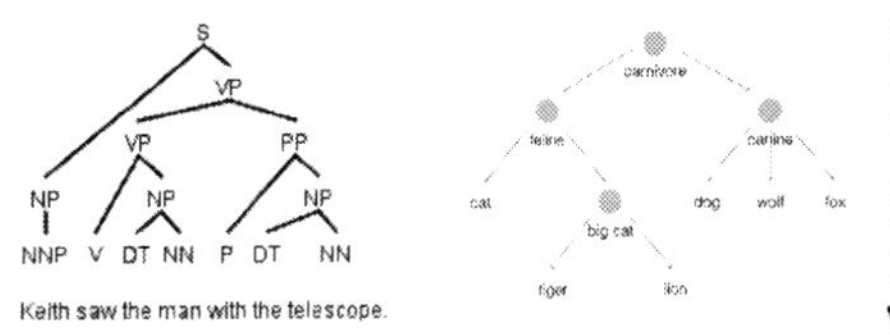

Figure 1: Two examples of hierarchical structure in natural language. **Left:** A constituent parse tree. **Right:** A fragment of WordNet. Arrows represent the direction in which the nodes become semantically more specific.

berlain et al., 2017). Hyperbolic spaces are non-Euclidean geometric spaces that naturally represent hierarchical relationships; for example, they can be viewed as continuous versions of trees (Krioukov et al., 2010). Indeed, Nickel and Kiela (2017) showed improved reconstruction error and link prediction when embedding WordNet and scientific collaboration networks into a hyperbolic space of small dimension compared to a Euclidean space of much larger dimension.

In this work, we explore the use of hyperbolic spaces for embedding natural language data, which has natural hierarchical structure in terms of *specificity*. For example, sub-phrases in a sentence can be arranged into a consituency-based parse tree where each node is semantically more specific than its parent (Figure 1 left). This hierarchical structure is not usually annotated in text corpora. Instead, we hypothesize that this structure is implicitly encoded in the range of natural language contexts in which a concept appears: semantically general concepts will occur in a wider range of contexts than semantically specific ones. We use this intuition to formulate unsupervised objectives for learning hyperbolic embeddings of text objects. By contrast, Nickel and Kiela (2017) only embedded graphs with an explicit hierarchical structure.

Proceedings of the Twelfth Workshop on Graph-Based Methods for Natural Language Processing (TextGraphs-12), pages 59–69
New Orleans, Louisiana, June 6, 2018. ©2018 Association for Computational Linguistics

Further, Nickel and Kiela (2017) only considered the non-parametric case where each object to be embedded is assigned its representation from a lookup table[1]. This approach is impractical for embedding natural language because there are too many sentences and phrases for such a table to fit in memory. For natural language, we must adopt a parametric approach where we learn the parameters θ of an encoder function f_θ that maps sequences of text to their embeddings. When training their non-parametric model, Nickel and Kiela (2017) relied on a projection step to keep their embeddings within their model of hyperbolic space. Specifically, they embedded their data in the Poincaré ball model of hyperbolic space, which consists of points in the unit ball $\mathcal{B}^d = \{\mathbf{x} \in \mathbb{R}^d : \|\mathbf{x}\| < 1\}$, but their Reimannian gradient-descent algorithm was not guaranteed to keep their embeddings within the unit ball. To address this issue, they applied a projection step after each gradient step to force the embeddings back into the unit ball, but this projection is not possible when the representations are the output of an encoder f_θ.

Our main contribution is to propose a simpler parametrization of hyperbolic embeddings that allows us to train parametric encoders. We avoid the need for a projection step by separately parameterizing the direction and norm of each embedding and applying a sigmoid activation function to the norm. This ensures that embeddings always satisfy $\|\mathbf{e}\| < 1$ (as required by the Poincaré ball model of hyperbolic space), even after arbitrary gradient steps. Once the embeddings are constrained in this way, all that is needed to induce hyperbolic embeddings is an appropriate distance metric (see Equation 1) in the loss function in place of the commonly used Euclidean or cosine distance metrics. In addition to allowing parametric encoders, this parameterization has an added benefit that instead of Riemannian-SGD (as used in Nickel and Kiela, 2017), we can use any of the popular optimization methods in deep learning, such as Adam (Kingma and Ba, 2014). We show that re-parameterizing in this manner leads to comparable reconstruction error to the method of Nickel and Kiela (2017) when learning non-parametric embeddings of WordNet.

We test our framework by learning unsupervised embeddings for two types of natural language data. First, we embed a graph of word co-occurrences extracted from a large text corpus. The resulting embeddings are hierarchically organized such that words occurring in many contexts are placed near the origin and words occurring in few contexts are placed near the boundary of the space. Using these embeddings, we see improved performance on a lexical entailment task, which supports our hypothesis that co-occurrence frequency is indicative of semantic specificity. However, this improvement comes at the cost of worse performance on a word similarity task. In the second experiment, we learn embeddings of sentences (and sub-sentence sequences) by applying the hyperbolic metric to a modified version of the Skip-Thoughts model (Kiros et al., 2015) that uses embeddings to predict local context in a text corpus. Since most sentences are unique, there is no clear notion of co-occurrence frequency in this case. However, we find a high correlation (0.67) between the norms of embedded constituent phrases from Penn Treebank (Marcus et al., 1993) and the height at which those phrases occur in their parse trees. We conclude that hyperbolic sentence embeddings encode some of the hierarchical structure represented by parse trees, without being trained to do so. However, experiments on downstream tasks do not show consistent improvements over baseline Euclidean embeddings.

2 Background – Poincaré Embeddings

In this section we give an overview of the Poincaré embeddings method from Nickel and Kiela (2017). A similar formulation was also presented in Chamberlain et al. (2017).

A hyperbolic space is a non-Euclidean geometric space obtained by replacing Euclid's parallel postulate with an alternative axiom. The parallel postulate asserts that for every line L and point P not on L, there is a unique line co-planar with P and L that passes through P and does not intersect L. In hyperbolic geometry, this axiom is replaced with the assertion that there are at least two such lines passing through P that do not intersect L (from which one can prove that there must be infinitely many such lines). In this geometry, some familiar properties of Euclidean space no longer hold; for example, the sum of interior angles in a triangle is less than 180 degrees. Like Euclidean geometry, hyperbolic geometry can be extended to

---

[1]Note that the term "non-parametric" has a different meaning here than in the case of Bayesian non-parametric statistics. Here it refers to the fact that the embeddings are not output by a parameterized function.

d-dimensions. d-dimensional hyperbolic space is unique up to a "curvature" constant $K<0$ that sets the length scale. Without loss of generality we assume $K=-1$.

In hyperbolic space, circle circumference ($2\pi \sinh r$) and disc area ($2\pi(\cosh r - 1)$) grow exponentially with radius, as opposed to Euclidean space where they only grow linearly and quadratically. This makes it particularly efficient to embed hierarchical structures like trees, where the number of nodes grows exponentially with depth (Krioukov et al., 2010). We hope that such embeddings will simultaneously capture both the similarity between objects (in their distances), and their relative depths in the hierarchy (in their norms).

There are several ways to model hyperbolic space within the more familiar Euclidean space. Of these, the Poincaré ball model is most suited for use with neural networks because its distance function is differentiable and it imposes a relatively simple constraint on the representations (Nickel and Kiela, 2017). Specifically, the Poincaré ball model consists of points within the unit ball $\mathcal{B}^d$, in which the distance between two points $\mathbf{u}, \mathbf{v} \in \mathcal{B}^d$ is

$$d(\mathbf{u}, \mathbf{v}) = \cosh^{-1}\left(1 + 2\frac{\|\mathbf{u} - \mathbf{v}\|^2}{(1 - \|\mathbf{u}\|^2)(1 - \|\mathbf{v}\|^2)}\right). \quad (1)$$

Notice that, as $\|\mathbf{u}\|$ approaches 1, its distance to almost all other points increases exponentially. Hence, an effective tree representation will place root nodes near the origin and leaf nodes near the boundary to ensure that root nodes are relatively close to all points while leaf nodes are relatively distant from most other leaf nodes.

In order to learn representations $\Theta = \{\theta_{\mathbf{i}}\}_{i=1}^n$ for a set of objects $\mathcal{S} = \{s_i\}_{i=1}^n$, we must define a loss function $\mathcal{L}(\Theta, d)$ that minimizes the hyperbolic distance between embeddings of similar objects and maximizes the hyperbolic distance between embeddings of different objects. Then we can solve the following optimization problem

$$\hat{\Theta} = \arg\min_{\Theta} \mathcal{L}(\Theta, d) \quad \text{s.t.} \quad \|\theta_{\mathbf{i}}\| < 1 \ \forall \theta_{\mathbf{i}} \in \Theta \quad (2)$$

Nickel and Kiela (2017) use Riemannian-SGD to optimize Equation 2. This involves computing the Riemannian gradient (which is a scaled version of the Euclidean gradient) with respect to the loss, performing a gradient-descent step, and projecting any embeddings that move out of $\mathcal{B}^d$ back within its boundary. In the following section, we propose a re-parametrization of Poincaré embeddings that removes the need for the projection step and allows the use of any of the popular optimization techniques in deep learning, such as Adam.

3 Parametric Poincaré Embeddings

Our goal is to learn a function $f : \mathcal{S} \to \mathcal{B}^d$ that maps objects from a set $\mathcal{S}$ to the Poincaré ball $\mathcal{B}^d$. However, the encoders typically used in deep learning, such as LSTMs, GRUs, and feedforward networks, may produce representations in arbitrary subspaces of $\mathbb{R}^{d'}$. We introduce a re-parameterization technique that maps $\mathbb{R}^{d'}$ to $\mathcal{B}^d$ and can be used on top of any existing encoder. Let $\mathbf{e}(s) \in \mathbb{R}^{d'}$ denote the output of the original encoder for a given $s \in \mathcal{S}$. The re-parameterization involves computing a direction vector $\mathbf{v}$ and a norm magnitude p from $\mathbf{e}(s)$ as follows:

$$\bar{\mathbf{v}} = \phi_{dir}(\mathbf{e}(s)), \quad \mathbf{v} = \frac{\bar{\mathbf{v}}}{\|\bar{\mathbf{v}}\|},$$

$$\bar{p} = \phi_{norm}(\mathbf{e}(s)), \quad p = \sigma(\bar{p}),$$

where $\phi_{dir} : \mathbb{R}^{d'} \to \mathbb{R}^d$, $\phi_{norm} : \mathbb{R}^{d'} \to \mathbb{R}$ can be arbitrary parametric functions, whose parameters will be optimized during training, and σ is the sigmoid function that ensures the resulting norm $p \in (0, 1)$. We will introduce specific instantiations of ϕ_{dir} and ϕ_{norm} in the subsections below. The re-parameterized embedding is defined as $\theta = p\mathbf{v}$, which lies in $\mathcal{B}^d$.

Let w denote the model parameters in $\mathbf{e}(s)$, ϕ_{dir}, and ϕ_{norm}. We wish to optimize a loss function $\mathcal{L}(w, d)$ that minimizes the hyperbolic distance d between embeddings of similar objects and maximizes the hyperbolic distance between embeddings of dissimilar objects. Since the embeddings θ are guaranteed to lie in $\mathcal{B}^d$, we can use any of the optimization methods popular in deep learning – we use Adam (Kingma and Ba, 2014).

Next we discuss specific instantiations of encoders, re-parameterization functions and loss functions for three types of problems.

3.1 Non-Parametric Supervised Embeddings

First, we test our re-parametrization by embedding the WordNet hierarchy with a non-parametric encoder – the same task considered by Nickel and Kiela (2017). The dataset is represented by a set of tuples $\mathcal{D} = \{(u, v)\}$, where each pair (u, v) denotes that u is a parent of v. Since u and v come from a fixed vocabulary of objects, we use a lookup table L as the base encoder, i.e, $\mathbf{e}(u) = L(u) \in \mathbb{R}^{d+1}$. We set $\phi_{dir} = \mathbf{x}_{1:d}$ and $\phi_{norm} = \mathbf{x}_{d+1}$ to be slicing functions that extract the first d and the $(d+1)$-th dimensions respectively.

We use the same loss function as Nickel and Kiela (2017), which uses negative samples $\mathcal{N}(u) = \{v : (u, v) \notin \mathcal{D}, v \neq u\}$ to maximize distance between embeddings of unrelated objects:

$$\mathcal{L}(w, d) = -\sum_{(u,v) \in \mathcal{D}} \log \frac{e^{-d(u,v)}}{\sum_{v' \in \mathcal{N}(u) \cup \{v\}} e^{-d(u,v')}}.$$

Note that this loss function makes no use of the direction of the edge (u, v), because $d(u, v)$ is symmetric. Nevertheless, we expect it to recover the hierarchical structure of $\mathcal{D}$.

3.2 Non-Parametric Unsupervised Word Embeddings

Next, we consider the problem of embedding words from a vocabulary $\mathcal{S}_\mathcal{V}$ given a text corpus $\mathcal{T} = (w_1, \ldots, w_{|\mathcal{T}|})$, where $w_i \in \mathcal{S}_\mathcal{V}$.

Traditional unsupervised methods, like word2vec (Mikolov et al., 2013b) and GloVe (Pennington et al., 2014), are optimized for preserving semantic similarity: the embeddings of similar words should be close, and the embeddings of semantically different words should be distant. Remarkably, these unsupervised embeddings also exhibit structural regularities, such as vector offsets corresponding to male-to-female or singular-to-plural transformations (Mikolov et al., 2013c,b). In this work, by embedding in hyperbolic space, we hope to encode both semantic similarity (in the hyperbolic distances between embeddings) and semantic specificity (in the hyperbolic norms of embeddings). Our hypothesis is that words denoting more general concepts will appear in varied contexts and hence will be placed closer to the origin – similar to how nodes close to the root in WordNet are placed close to the origin in Nickel and Kiela (2017). Tasks that rely on a hierarchical relationship between words might benefit from embeddings with these properties.

The idea of using specialized vector space models for encoding various lexical relations was previously explored by Henderson and Popa (2016). While they looked exclusively at the entailment relation, the notion we study here is that of *semantic specificity*, which is more general but also difficult to define formally. One example is that "musician" is related to "music" and more specific than it, but not necessarily entailed by it.

Both word2vec and GloVe embed words using co-occurrences of pairs of words occur within a fixed window size in $\mathcal{T}$. Here, we construct a co-occurrence graph $\mathcal{G} = \{(w, v)\}$ that consists of all pairs of words that occur within a fixed window of each other. Certain pairs co-occur more frequently than others, and we preserve this information by allowing repeated edges in $\mathcal{G}$: each pair (w, v) occurs f^c times in $\mathcal{G}$, where f is the frequency of that pair in $\mathcal{T}$ and $c < 1$ is a downsampling constant. We embed $\mathcal{G}$ in the Poincaré ball in the manner described in Section 3.1.

3.3 Parametric Unsupervised Sentence Embeddings

Finally, we consider embedding longer units of text such as sentences and phrases. We denote the set of all multi-word expressions of interest as $\mathcal{S}_\mathcal{Z}$. Our goal is to learn an encoder function $f : \mathcal{S}_\mathcal{Z} \to \mathcal{B}^d$ in an unsupervised manner from a text corpus $\mathcal{T} = (s_1, \ldots, s_{|\mathcal{T}|})$, where $s_i \in \mathcal{S}_\mathcal{Z}$.

Sentence embeddings are motivated by the phenomenal success of word embeddings as general purpose feature representations for a variety of downstream tasks. The desiderata of multi-word embeddings are similar to those of word embeddings: semantically similar units should be close to each other in embedding space, and complex semantic properties should map to geometric properties in the embedding space. Our hypothesis is that embedding multi-word units in hyperbolic space will capture the hierarchical structure of specificity of the meanings of these units.

We start with Skip-Thoughts (Kiros et al., 2015), an unsupervised model for sentence embeddings that is trained to predict sentences surrounding a source sentence from its representation. Skip-Thoughts consists of an encoder and two decoders, all of which are parameterized as Gated Recurrent Units (GRUs) (Cho et al., 2014). The encoder produces a fixed-size representation $f_\theta(s_i)$ for $s_i \in \mathcal{S}_\mathcal{Z}$, and the two decoders reconstruct the previous sentence s_{i-1} and the next sentence s_{i+1} in an identical manner, as follows:

$$\mathbf{h}_t = \text{GRU}(w_{<t}, f_\theta(s_i)),$$

$$P(w_t | w_{<t}, f_\theta(s_i)) \propto \exp(\mathbf{v}_{w_t}^T \mathbf{h}_t),$$

where $(w_1, \ldots, w_T)$ is the sequence of words

in s_{i-1} or s_{i+1} and $\mathbf{v}_w$ denotes an output embedding for w. The loss minimizes $-\sum_t \log P(w_t|w_{<t}, f_\theta(s_i))$.

In order to learn hyperbolic embeddings, the loss must depend directly on the hyperbolic distance between the source and target embeddings. As an intermediate step, we present a modified version of Skip-Thoughts where we remove the GRU from the decoding step and instead directly predict a bag-of-words surrounding the source sentence, as follows:

$$\mathbf{c}_t = \frac{1}{2K} \sum_{k=1}^{K} \mathbf{v}'_{w_{t-k}} + \mathbf{v}'_{w_{t+k}},$$

$$P(w_t|w_{\neq t}, f_\theta(s_i)) \propto \exp\left(\mathbf{v}_{w_t}^T f_\theta(s_i) + \mathbf{v}_{w_t}^T \mathbf{c}_t\right).$$

Here, $\mathbf{c}_t$ is an average word embedding of the bi-directional local context around the word to be predicted. We found it was important to condition the prediction on $\mathbf{c}_t$ in order to learn a good quality encoder model f_θ, since it can take care of uninteresting language modeling effects. Empirically, the sentence encoder trained in this manner gives around 1% lower average performance on downstream tasks (discussed in Section 4.3) than the original Skip-Thoughts model, while being considerably faster. More importantly, the prediction probability now directly depends on the inner product between $\mathbf{v}_{w_t}$ and $f_\theta(s_i)$. We can now introduce a hyperbolic version of the likelihood as follows:

$$P(w_t|w_{\neq t}, f_\theta(s_i)) \propto$$
$$\exp\left(-\lambda_1 d(\mathbf{v}_{w_t}, f_\theta(s_i)) - \lambda_2 d(\mathbf{v}_{w_t}, \mathbf{c}_t)\right).$$

Here, d is the hyperbolic distance function (Equation 1) and λ_1, λ_2 are learned coefficients that control the importance of the two terms. After training, we observed that $\lambda_2 > \lambda_1$, which supports our intuition that local context is more important in predicting a word.

To ensure that $\mathbf{v}_{w_t}, f_\theta(s_i), \mathbf{c}_t \in \mathcal{B}^d$, we use the following parameterization:

$$\phi_{dir}(\mathbf{x}) = W_1^T \mathbf{x}, \quad \phi_{norm}(\mathbf{x}) = W_2^T \mathbf{x},$$

where $\mathbf{x} = \{\hat{\mathbf{v}}_{w_t}, \hat{\mathbf{c}}_t, \hat{f}_\theta(s_i)\}$; $\hat{\mathbf{v}}_{w_t}$ is the Euclidean output embedding for word w_t, obtained from a lookup table; $\hat{\mathbf{c}}_t$ is the Euclidean local context embedding, obtained by averaging Euclidean word vectors from a window around w_t; and $\hat{f}_\theta$ is a bidi-

Method		Dim		
		5	20	100
From Nickel and Kiela (2017)				
Euclidean	Rank	3542.3	1685.9	1187.3
	MAP	0.024	0.087	0.162
Poincaré	Rank	4.9	3.8	3.9
	MAP	0.823	0.855	0.857
This work				
Poincaré (re-parameterized)	Rank	10.7	6.3	5.5
	MAP	0.736	0.875	0.818

Table 1: Reconstruction errors for various embedding dimensions on WordNet.

rectional GRU encoder over the words of s_i:

$$\mathbf{h}_T^f = \overrightarrow{\text{GRU}}(s_i), \quad \mathbf{h}_1^b = \overleftarrow{\text{GRU}}(s_i)$$
$$\hat{f}_\theta(s_i) = \mathbf{h}_T^f \| \mathbf{h}_1^b$$

Similar to Skip-Thoughts, the loss minimizes $-\sum_t \log P(w_t|w_{\neq t}, f_\theta(s_i))$.

4 Experiments & Results

4.1 WordNet

The WordNet noun hierarchy is a collection of tuples $\mathcal{D} = \{(u, v)\}$, where each pair (u, v) denotes that u is a hypernym of v. Following Nickel and Kiela (2017), we learned embeddings using the transitive closure $\mathcal{D}^+$, which consists of 82,114 nouns and 743,241 hypernym-hyponym edges. We compared our results to the original method from Nickel and Kiela (2017) across three different embedding sizes. In each case, we evaluated the embeddings by attempting to reconstruct the WordNet tree using the nearest neighbors of the nodes. For each node, we retrieved a ranked list of its nearest neighbors in embedding space and computed the *mean rank* of its ground truth children, and also computed the *Mean Average Precision* (MAP), which is the average precision at the threshold of each correctly retrieved child. Results are presented in Table 1.

The re-parameterized Poincaré embeddings method has comparable reconstruction error to the original Poincaré method, whereas both are significantly superior to the Euclidean embeddings method. Figure 2 shows reconstruction error after each epoch when training the original and re-parameterized Poincaré embeddings, along with the elapsed wall time in minutes[2]. The

---

[2]For the original method we used the official code release at `https://github.com/facebookresearch/`

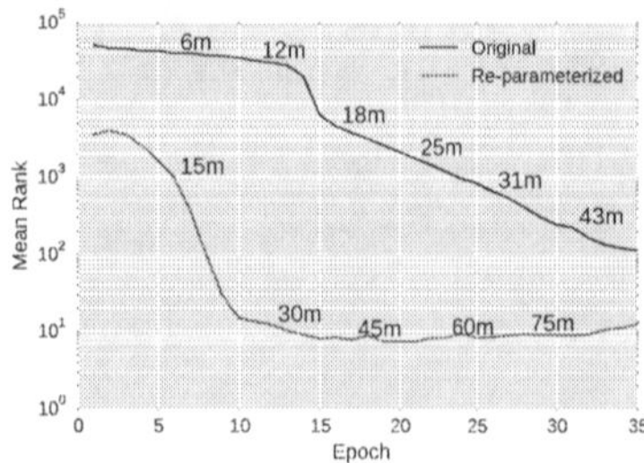

Figure 2: Mean Rank for reconstructing the WordNet graph after each training epoch (up to epoch 35) for the original Poincaré embeddings method (Nickel and Kiela, 2017) and our re-parameterized version. Wall time elapsed in minutes is also shown against the curves. Dimension $d = 10$.

Word	Nearest neighbors
vapor	boiling, melting, evaporation, cooling, vapour
towering	eruptions, tsunamis, hotspots, himalayas, volcanic
mercedes	dmg, benz, porsche, clk, mclaren
forties	twenties, thirties, roaring, koniuchy, inhabitant
eruption	caldera, vents, calderas, limnic, volcano
palladium	boron, anion, uranium, ceric, hexafluoride
employment	incentives, benefits, financial, incentive, investment
weighed	tonnes, weigh, weighs, kilograms, weighing

Table 2: Nearest Neighbors in terms of cosine distance for Poincaré embeddings of words ($d = 20$).

re-parameterized method converges much faster, with its best error achieved around epoch 20, compared to the original method that reaches its best error after hundreds of epochs. This is despite using a larger batch size of 1024 for the re-parameterized method than the original method, which uses batch size 50. We hypothesize that the speed-up is largely due to using the Adam optimizer which is made possible by the fact that the re-parameterization ensures the embeddings always lie within the Poincaré ball.

4.2 Word Embeddings

We used the TEXT8 corpus[3] to evaluate our technique for learning non-parametric unsupervised word embeddings (Section 3.2). Though small (17M tokens), the TEXT8 corpus is a useful benchmark for quickly comparing embedding methods.

For hyperbolic embeddings, the nearest neigh-

poincare-embeddings with the recommended hyperparameter settings. Our re-parameterized model is implemented in TensorFlow (Abadi et al., 2016). Wall time was recorded on a CPU with 8-core AMD Opteron 6376 Processor.

[3] http://mattmahoney.net/dc/text8.zip

bors of most words by hyperbolic distance (Equation 1) are all uninteresting common words (e.g. numbers, quantifiers, etc), because points near the origin are relatively close to all points, whereas distances between points increases exponentially as the points approach the boundary of $\mathcal{B}^d$. Instead, we find nearest neighbors in hyperbolic space using cosine distance, which is motivated by the fact that the Poincaré ball model is conformal: angles between vectors are identical to their Euclidean counterparts. Some nearest neighbors of hyperbolic word embeddings are shown in Table 2. The closest neighbors typically represent one of several semantic relations with the query word. For example, "boiling" produces "vapor", "towering" is a quality of "eruptions", "dmg" is the parent company of "mercedes", "tonnes" is a measure of "weighed", and so on. This is a consequence of embedding the word-cooccurrence graph, which implicitly represents these relations.

Table 3 shows lists of related words that contain a particular substring in order of increasing hyperbolic norm. We also show the counts in the corpus of these words, which are correlated to the number of contexts they occur in. As expected, words occurring in fewer contexts have higher hyperbolic norm, and this corresponds to increased specificity as we move down the list; for example "bulldogs" has a higher norm than "dog", and "greatest" has a higher norm than "great". The Spearman correlation between $1/f$, where f is the frequency of a word in the corpus, and the norm of the embedding is 0.77.

We quantitatively evaluate hyperbolic embeddings on two tasks against the baseline Skip-Gram with Negative Sampling (SGNS) embeddings (Mikolov et al., 2013a)[4]. The first task is Word-Similarity on the WordSim-353 dataset (Finkelstein et al., 2001), which measures whether the embeddings preserve semantic similarity between words as judged by humans. We compute Spearman's correlation between ground truth similarity scores and cosine distances in embedding space between all pairs of words in the dataset. The second task is HyperLex (Vulić et al., 2017), which measures the extent to which embeddings preserve lexical entailment relationships of the form "X is a type of Y". These are precisely the

[4] We use the code available at https://github.com/tensorflow/models/tree/master/tutorials/embedding, which was tuned for the TEXT8 corpus.

"bank"			"music"			"dog"			"great"		
Word	Count	Norm	Word	Count	Norm	Word	Count	Norm	Word	Count	Norm
bank	1076	2.56	music	4470	1.58	dog	566	3.21	great	4784	2.11
bankruptcy	106	4.61	musical	1265	2.56	dogs	184	4.27	greater	1502	2.51
banking	185	5.92	musicians	435	4.07	dogme	16	6.52	greatest	753	2.97
bankrupt	28	5.93	musician	413	4.32	bulldogs	8	7.08	greatly	530	3.46
banks	407	6.45	musicals	38	5.76	endogenous	5	7.55	greatness	12	6.41
banknote	13	6.62	musicology	18	6.38	sheepdog	5	7.73			

Table 3: Words in order of increasing hyperbolic norm which contain the substring indicated in the top row. Their counts in the TEXT8 corpus are also shown. Dimension size $d = 20$.

Task	Method	Dimension			
		5	20	50	100
WordSim-353	SGNS	0.350	0.566	0.676	0.689
	Poincaré	0.305	0.451	0.451	0.455
HyperLex	SGNS	-0.002	0.093	0.124	0.140
	Poincaré	0.259	0.246	0.246	0.248

Table 4: Spearman's ρ correlation coefficient for Word Similarity and Lexical Entailment tasks using SGNS and Poincaré embeddings of various sizes.

Sentence	Norm
a creaky staircase gothic .	6.21
it 's a rare window on an artistic collaboration .	6.32
a dopey movie clothed in excess layers of hipness .	6.35
an imponderably stilted and self-consciously arty movie .	6.65
there's a delightfully quirky movie ... , but brooms isn't it .	6.83
a trifle of a movie, with a few laughs ... unremarkable soft center .	6.86

Table 5: Sentences from Movie Reviews dataset with their norms. Each row represents a nearest neighbor to and with a greater norm than the sentence in the row above.

kind of relations we hope to capture in the norm of hyperbolic embeddings. Given a pair (x, y) of words, we compute the score for the relationship is-a(x, y) in the same way as Nickel and Kiela (2017):

$$\text{score(is-a}(x, y)) = -(1 + \alpha(\|y\| - \|x\|))d(x, y).$$

If x and y are close and $\|y\| < \|x\|$, the above score will be positive, implying x is a type of y.

Table 4 shows the scores on these two tasks for both SGNS and Poincaré embeddings for various embedding sizes. SGNS embeddings are superior for preserving word similarities, while Poincaré embeddings are superior for preserving lexical entailment. However, the best score for Poincaré embeddings is only 0.259, which is quite low. In comparison to the unsupervised baselines studied in Vulić et al. (2017), Poincaré embeddings rank second behind the simple Frequency Ratio baseline which, achieves 0.279[5].

4.3 Sentence Embeddings

We use the BookCorpus (Zhu et al., 2015) to learn sentence and phrase embeddings. We pre-process the data into triples of the form (s_{i-1}, s_i, s_{i+1}) consisting of both full sentences, as in the original Skip-Thoughts model, and sub-sentence sequences of words sampled according to the same lengths as sentences in the corpus. We found that

augmenting the dataset in this manner led to consistent improvements on downstream tasks.

Similar to word embeddings, we expect that sentence (phrase) embeddings will be organized in a hierarchical manner such that sentences (phrases) that appear in a variety of contexts are closer to the origin. However, unlike word embeddings where we could compare hyperbolic norm to frequency in the corpus, this effect is hard to measure directly for sentences (phrases) because most only appear a small number of times in the corpus. Instead, we check whether the embeddings exhibit a known hierarchical structure: constituent parses of sentences. We take Section 23 from the Wall Street Journal subset of Penn Treebank (Marcus et al., 1993), which is annotated with gold standard constituent parse tree structures, and embed each node from each tree using the learned parametric encoder f_θ. The Spearman correlation between the norm of the resulting embedding and the height of the node in its tree, computed over all nodes in the set, is 0.671. Figure 3 shows some example parses with the hyperbolic norm at each node. The norms generally increase as we move upwards, indicating that the learned embeddings encode some of this particular form of hierarchical structure. Table 5 shows examples from the Movie Review corpus (Pang et al., 2002), in which we generated a chain of sentences with increasing norm by iteratively searching for the nearest neighbor with norm greater than the previous sentence.

---

[5]This does not include baselines that use extra information like WordNet while learning the embeddings.

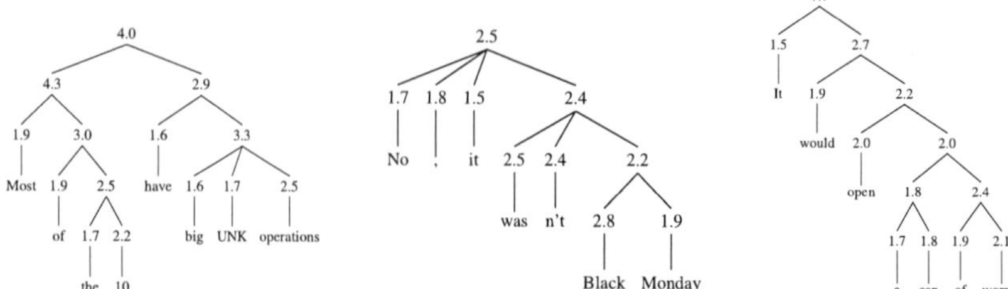

Figure 3: Constituent parse trees from the Penn Treebank with hyperbolic norms of the phrase embeddings at each node.

Encoder Dim	Word Dim	Method	Perplexity	CR	SUBJ	MPQA	MR	MultiNLI	SNLI
10	100	Euclidean	117	0.639	0.582	0.689	0.546	0.419	0.483
		Poincaré	110	0.640	0.623	0.769	0.534	0.417	0.480
100	200	Euclidean	61	0.719	0.882	0.823	0.694	0.534	0.692
		Poincaré	53	0.722	0.890	0.848	0.696	0.537	0.684
1000	620	Euclidean	61	0.804	0.925	0.860	0.742	0.617	0.741
		Poincaré	46	0.792	0.921	0.880	0.746	0.620	0.746
2400	620	Skip-Thoughts	$-^*$	0.836	0.938	0.889	0.795	0.650	0.766

Table 6: Held out set perplexity and downstream task performance for sentence embeddings of various sizes. *Perplexity of the Skip-Thoughts model is not comparable to our methods since it only uses uni-directional local context.

Next, following common practice for evaluating sentence representations, we evaluate the trained Poincaré encoder as a black-box feature extractor for downstream tasks. We choose four binary classification benchmarks from the original Skip-Thoughts evaluation – CR, MR, MPQA and SUBJ – and two entailment tasks – MultiNLI (Williams et al., 2017) and SNLI (Bowman et al., 2015). For the binary classification tasks we train SVM models with a kernel based on hyperbolic distance between sentences, and for the entailment tasks we train multi-layer perceptrons on top of the premise and hypothesis embeddings and their element-wise products and differences. As a baseline, we compare to embeddings trained using the Euclidean distance metric. Table 6 reports the results of these evaluations for various embedding dimensions. Poincaré embeddings achieve a lower perplexity in each case, suggesting a more efficient use of the embedding space. However, both sets of embeddings perform similarly on downstream tasks, except for the MPQA opinion polarity task where Poincaré embeddings do significantly better. Training with embedding sizes greater than 1000 did not show any further improvements in our experiments.

4.4 Discussion

The goal of this work was to explore whether hyperbolic spaces are useful for learning embeddings of natural language data. Ultimately, the useful-ness of an embedding method depends on its performance on downstream tasks of interest. In that respect we found mixed results in our evaluation. For word embeddings, we found that hyperbolic embeddings preserve co-occurrence frequency information in their norms, and this leads to improved performance on a lexical entailment task. However, decreased performance on a word similarity task means that these embeddings may not be useful across all tasks. In general, this suggests that different architectures are needed for capturing different types of lexical relations. We experimented with several other loss functions, preprocessing techniques and hyper-parameter settings, which we did not describe in this paper due to space constraints, but the conclusions remained the same.

For sentence embeddings, we found evidence that hyperbolic embeddings preserve phrase constituency information in their norms. A deeper investigation of the learned hierarchy is difficult since our encoder is a parametric function over a (practically) infinite set and there is no clear notion of edges in the learned embeddings. On downstream tasks, we saw a small improvement over the Euclidean baseline in some cases and a small degradation in others, again highlighting the need for specialized embeddings for different tasks. We hope that our initial study can pave the way for more work on the applicability of the hyperbolic metric for learning useful embeddings of natural language data.

5 Related Work

Tay et al. (2018) used the hyperbolic distance metric to learn question and answer embeddings on the Poincaré ball for question-answer retrieval. The main difference to our work is that we explore unsupervised objectives for learning generic word and sentence representations from a text corpus. Furthermore, we show that by using re-parameterization instead of projection to constrain the embeddings, we can view the distance metric as any other non-linear layer in a deep network and remove the need for Riemannian-SGD.

Several works have attempted to learn hierarchical word embeddings. Order Embeddings (Vendrov et al., 2015) and LEAR (Vulić and Mrkšić, 2017) are supervised methods that also encode hierarchy information in the norm of the embeddings by adding regularization terms to the loss function. In comparison, our method is unsupervised. HyperVec (Nguyen et al., 2017) is a supervised method which ensures that the hypernymy relation is assigned a higher similarity score in the learned embeddings than other relations such as synonymy. The vector space model for distribution semantics introduced by Henderson and Popa (2016) is unsupervised and re-interprets word2vec embeddings to predict entailment relations between pairs of words. DIVE (Chang et al., 2017) is also unsupervised, and achieves a score of 32.6% on the lexical entailment task, but it is unclear how well the embeddings preserve semantic similarity.

For sentence embeddings, several works have looked at improved loss functions for Skip-Thoughts to make the model faster and light-weight (Tang et al., 2017c,a,b). Ba et al. (2016) introduced a layer normalization method that shows consistent improvements when included in the GRU layers in Skip-Thoughts, and we used this in our encoder. More recently, improved sentence representations were obtained using discourse based objectives (Jernite et al., 2017; Nie et al., 2017) and using supervision from natural language inference data (Conneau et al., 2017).

6 Conclusion

We presented a re-parameterization method that allows us to learn Poincaré embeddings on top of arbitrary encoder modules using arbitrary distance-based loss functions. We showed that this re-parameterization leads to comparable performance to the original method from Nickel and Kiela (2017) when explicit hierarchical structure is present in the data. When we applied this method to natural language data at the word- and sentence-level, we found evidence of intuitive notions of hierarchy in the learned embeddings. This led to improvements on some – but not all – downstream tasks. Future work could either focus on alternative formulations for unsupervised hyperbolic embeddings, or alternative downstream tasks where hierarchical organization may be more useful.

References

Martín Abadi, Paul Barham, Jianmin Chen, Zhifeng Chen, Andy Davis, Jeffrey Dean, Matthieu Devin, Sanjay Ghemawat, Geoffrey Irving, Michael Isard, et al. 2016. Tensorflow: A system for large-scale machine learning. In *OSDI*, volume 16, pages 265–283.

Aaron B Adcock, Blair D Sullivan, and Michael W Mahoney. 2013. Tree-like structure in large social and information networks. In *Data Mining (ICDM), 2013 IEEE 13th International Conference on*, pages 1–10. IEEE.

Jimmy Lei Ba, Jamie Ryan Kiros, and Geoffrey E Hinton. 2016. Layer normalization. *arXiv preprint arXiv:1607.06450*.

Samuel R. Bowman, Gabor Angeli, Christopher Potts, and Christopher D. Manning. 2015. A large annotated corpus for learning natural language inference. In *Proceedings of the 2015 Conference on Empirical Methods in Natural Language Processing (EMNLP)*. Association for Computational Linguistics.

Benjamin Paul Chamberlain, James Clough, and Marc Peter Deisenroth. 2017. Neural embeddings of graphs in hyperbolic space. *arXiv preprint arXiv:1705.10359*.

Haw-Shiuan Chang, ZiYun Wang, Luke Vilnis, and Andrew McCallum. 2017. Distributional inclusion vector embedding for unsupervised hypernymy detection. *arXiv preprint arXiv:1710.00880*.

Kyunghyun Cho, Bart van Merriënboer, Çalar Gülçehre, Dzmitry Bahdanau, Fethi Bougares, Holger Schwenk, and Yoshua Bengio. 2014. Learning phrase representations using rnn encoder–decoder for statistical machine translation. In *Proceedings of the 2014 Conference on Empirical Methods in Natural Language Processing (EMNLP)*, pages 1724–

1734, Doha, Qatar. Association for Computational Linguistics.

Alexis Conneau, Douwe Kiela, Holger Schwenk, Loïc Barrault, and Antoine Bordes. 2017. Supervised learning of universal sentence representations from natural language inference data. In *Proceedings of the 2017 Conference on Empirical Methods in Natural Language Processing*, pages 670–680. Association for Computational Linguistics.

Martin BH Everaert, Marinus AC Huybregts, Noam Chomsky, Robert C Berwick, and Johan J Bolhuis. 2015. Structures, not strings: linguistics as part of the cognitive sciences. *Trends in cognitive sciences*, 19(12):729–743.

Lev Finkelstein, Evgeniy Gabrilovich, Yossi Matias, Ehud Rivlin, Zach Solan, Gadi Wolfman, and Eytan Ruppin. 2001. Placing search in context: The concept revisited. In *Proceedings of the 10th international conference on World Wide Web*, pages 406–414. ACM.

James Henderson and Diana Popa. 2016. A vector space for distributional semantics for entailment. In *Proceedings of the 54th Annual Meeting of the Association for Computational Linguistics (Volume 1: Long Papers)*, pages 2052–2062. Association for Computational Linguistics.

Yacine Jernite, Samuel R Bowman, and David Sontag. 2017. Discourse-based objectives for fast unsupervised sentence representation learning. *arXiv preprint arXiv:1705.00557*.

Diederik P Kingma and Jimmy Ba. 2014. Adam: A method for stochastic optimization. In *Proceedings of the 3rd International Conference on Learning Representations (ICLR)*.

Ryan Kiros, Yukun Zhu, Ruslan R Salakhutdinov, Richard Zemel, Raquel Urtasun, Antonio Torralba, and Sanja Fidler. 2015. Skip-thought vectors. In *Advances in neural information processing systems*, pages 3294–3302.

Dmitri Krioukov, Fragkiskos Papadopoulos, Maksim Kitsak, Amin Vahdat, and Marián Boguná. 2010. Hyperbolic geometry of complex networks. *Physical Review E*, 82(3):036106.

Mitchell P Marcus, Mary Ann Marcinkiewicz, and Beatrice Santorini. 1993. Building a large annotated corpus of english: The penn treebank. *Computational linguistics*, 19(2):313–330.

Tomas Mikolov, Kai Chen, Greg Corrado, and Jeffrey Dean. 2013a. Efficient estimation of word representations in vector space. *arXiv preprint arXiv:1301.3781*.

Tomas Mikolov, Ilya Sutskever, Kai Chen, Greg S Corrado, and Jeff Dean. 2013b. Distributed representations of words and phrases and their compositionality. In *Advances in neural information processing systems*, pages 3111–3119.

Tomas Mikolov, Wen-tau Yih, and Geoffrey Zweig. 2013c. Linguistic regularities in continuous space word representations. In *Proceedings of the 2013 Conference of the North American Chapter of the Association for Computational Linguistics: Human Language Technologies*, pages 746–751.

Kim Anh Nguyen, Maximilian Köper, Sabine Schulte im Walde, and Ngoc Thang Vu. 2017. Hierarchical embeddings for hypernymy detection and directionality. In *Proceedings of the 2017 Conference on Empirical Methods in Natural Language Processing*, pages 233–243. Association for Computational Linguistics.

Maximillian Nickel and Douwe Kiela. 2017. Poincaré embeddings for learning hierarchical representations. In I. Guyon, U. V. Luxburg, S. Bengio, H. Wallach, R. Fergus, S. Vishwanathan, and R. Garnett, editors, *Advances in Neural Information Processing Systems 30*, pages 6338–6347. Curran Associates, Inc.

Allen Nie, Erin D Bennett, and Noah D Goodman. 2017. Dissent: Sentence representation learning from explicit discourse relations. *arXiv preprint arXiv:1710.04334*.

Bo Pang, Lillian Lee, and Shivakumar Vaithyanathan. 2002. Thumbs up?: sentiment classification using machine learning techniques. In *Proceedings of the ACL-02 conference on Empirical methods in natural language processing-Volume 10*, pages 79–86. Association for Computational Linguistics.

Jeffrey Pennington, Richard Socher, and Christopher Manning. 2014. Glove: Global vectors for word representation. In *Proceedings of the 2014 conference on empirical methods in natural language processing (EMNLP)*, pages 1532–1543.

Shuai Tang, Hailin Jin, Chen Fang, Zhaowen Wang, and Virginia de Sa. 2017a. Rethinking skip-thought: A neighborhood based approach. In *Proceedings of the 2nd Workshop on Representation Learning for NLP*, pages 211–218. Association for Computational Linguistics.

Shuai Tang, Hailin Jin, Chen Fang, Zhaowen Wang, and Virginia R de Sa. 2017b. Exploring asymmetric encoder-decoder structure for context-based sentence representation learning. *arXiv preprint arXiv:1710.10380*.

Shuai Tang, Hailin Jin, Chen Fang, Zhaowen Wang, and Virginia R de Sa. 2017c. Trimming and improving skip-thought vectors. *arXiv preprint arXiv:1706.03148*.

Yi Tay, Luu Anh Tuan, and Siu Cheung Hui. 2018. Hyperbolic representation learning for fast and efficient neural question answering. In *Proceedings of the Eleventh ACM International Conference on Web Search and Data Mining*, WSDM '18, pages 583–591, New York, NY, USA. ACM.

Ivan Vendrov, Ryan Kiros, Sanja Fidler, and Raquel Urtasun. 2015. Order-embeddings of images and language. *arXiv preprint arXiv:1511.06361*.

Ivan Vulić, Daniela Gerz, Douwe Kiela, Felix Hill, and Anna Korhonen. 2017. Hyperlex: A large-scale evaluation of graded lexical entailment. *Computational Linguistics*, 43(4):781–835.

Ivan Vulić and Nikola Mrkšić. 2017. Specialising word vectors for lexical entailment. *arXiv preprint arXiv:1710.06371*.

Adina Williams, Nikita Nangia, and Samuel R Bowman. 2017. A broad-coverage challenge corpus for sentence understanding through inference. *arXiv preprint arXiv:1704.05426*.

Yukun Zhu, Ryan Kiros, Rich Zemel, Ruslan Salakhutdinov, Raquel Urtasun, Antonio Torralba, and Sanja Fidler. 2015. Aligning books and movies: Towards story-like visual explanations by watching movies and reading books. In *Proceedings of the IEEE international conference on computer vision*, pages 19–27.

A Implementation Details

A.1 WordNet Experiments

For our re-parameterized Poincaré embeddings we used a batch size 1024, learning rate 0.005, and no burn-in period. The loss was optimized using the Adam optimizer. Embeddings were initialized in $\mathcal{U}[-0.001, 0.001]$. We sampled 10 negatives on the fly during training independently for each positive sample. We clipped gradients to a norm of 5. Embeddings were initialized to a small norm around $\sigma(-5)$.

A.2 Word Embedding Experiments

The TEXT8 corpus contains around 17M tokens preprocessed such that all tokens are lowercase, numbers are spelled out, and any characters not in a-z are replaced by whitespace. We removed stopwords and constructed the word-cooccurrence graph $\mathcal{G}$ by adding an edge between words appearing within 5 tokens of each other in the resulting corpus. We used $c = 0.25$ for subsampling frequent edges, and trained our embedding model using the Adam optimizer with batch size 512 and learning rate 0.005. We sampled 50 negatives per step for the loss. We initialized the norms of the word embeddings around $\sigma(-5)$. All hyperparameters were tuned to maximize performance on the word similarity task.

A.3 Sentence Embedding Experiments

During preprocessing, only the top 20,000 most frequent types were retained and the rest were replaced with the UNK type. We optimized the loss function using Adam optimizer with a batch size of 64. The initial learning rate was tuned between $0.005, 0.0008, 0.0001$ which was then decayed exponentially to half its value in 100,000 steps. When decoding we utilize a local context from a window of $K = 2$ words around the target word. The embedding norms are initialized around $\sigma(-2)$.

Author Index

Agrawal, Amol, 38

Chang, Haw-Shiuan, 38
Chen, Guangliang, 28

Dahl, George, 59
Dai, Andrew, 59
Desai, Anirudha, 38
Dhingra, Bhuwan, 59

Ganesh, Ananya, 38
Gouveia da Silva, Thiago, 18

Hahn-Powell, Gus, 1
Hough, Alfred, 38
Huet, Stéphane, 18

Jansen, Peter, 12

Linhares Pontes, Elvys, 18
Linhares, Andréa carneiro, 18
Luo, Fan, 1

Malliaros, Fragkiskos, 49
Mathur, Vinayak, 38
McCallum, Andrew, 38

Norouzi, Mohammad, 59

Pham, Khiem, 28

Shallue, Christopher, 59
Skianis, Konstantinos, 49
Surdeanu, Mihai, 1

Torres-Moreno, Juan-Manuel, 18

Valenzuela-Escárcega, Marco A., 1
Vazirgiannis, Michalis, 49

Yin, Ruiqing, 7

Zhang, Zheng, 7
Zweigenbaum, Pierre, 7